Atheist Priest?
Don Cupitt and Christianity

Scott Cowdell

ATHEIST PRIEST?
Don Cupitt and Christianity

SCM PRESS LTD

British Library Cataloguing in Publication Data

Cowdell, Scott
   Atheist priest?
   1. Christian theology. Cupitt, Don
   I. Title
   230'.092'4

   ISBN 0–334–00003–3

First published 1988
by SCM Press Ltd,
26–30 Tottenham Road, London N1 4BZ

Typeset at The Spartan Press Ltd,
Lymington, Hants
and printed in Great Britain by
Richard Clay Ltd, Bungay, Suffolk

To friends made at
St Francis' Theological College, Brisbane,
in memory of five happy years
COLLABORANTES FIDE EVANGELII

As far as could be learnt it appeared that the poor young dog, still under the impression that since he was kept for running after sheep, the more he ran after them the better, had . . . collected all the ewes into a corner, driven the timid creatures through the hedge, across the upper field, and by main force of worrying had given them momentum enough to break down a portion of the rotten railing, and so hurled them over the edge. (He) . . . had done his work so thoroughly that he was considered too good a workman to live, and was, in fact, taken and tragically shot at twelve o'clock that same day – another instance of the untoward fate which so often attends dogs and other philosophers who follow out a train of reasoning to its logical conclusion, and attempt perfectly consistent conduct in a world made up so largely of compromise.

Thomas Hardy, *Far From The Madding Crowd*

Contents

Foreword by Don Cupitt

Scott Cowdell is a young Australian theologian currently working at the University of Queensland, and an Anglican deacon. His book is not the first to have been prompted by my writings, but it is the first study. Keith Ward (*Holding Fast to God*, SPCK 1982) and Brian Hebblethwaite (*The Ocean of Truth*, CUP 1988) wrote to refute me, and like other commentators they refer only to my work of the early 1980s. They were not concerned to ask either how I reached the early-eighties views or why I have since moved away from them. Scott Cowdell has sought to fill the gap by drawing up what must be a very-nearly complete list of my publications 1961–1987, and from them reconstructing the development of my thinking.

In this he got little help from me. I have been in such a hurry these past dozen years or so that I had no bibliography to offer him, and only a rather hazy picture of the route I had taken. As it turns out, Cowdell's reconstruction rightly points out numerous warts, loose ends, blind alleys and forced retractations, as well as various long-term preoccupations. He quotes the themes of God, Christ, theological realism, the end of the world, ethics and liberalism. I add two others: the first is a concern for language which has led me at different times to be interested in analogy, regulative truth, the rhetoric of Jesus, expressivism and, most recently, post-structuralist theories of meaning and interpretation. The second is something of a family trait: an extreme love of freedom, which has led me to take up the ideas of spiritual mobility, travelling light, the Negative Way and anti-philosophy.

In these two areas, I have gone through some odd gyrations and transformations. However, I said from the first that the truth is in the movement – and that (by the way) is doubtless why I am so bad at answering criticisms. By the time they have come in I have moved on; and in any case I do not share the linguistic scientism of those who think in terms of attacking and defending formalized 'positions'. My critics are disciples of Socrates: they seem to want to stop and dissect an essence or two in order to determine precisely which of us is right, whereas I want to say you can't do that. Meanings don't stay still for long enough.

The whole question of movement has itself moved oddly. In the late 1960s I hoped to move from grossly inadequate to less inadequate images of God. The trail of broken images would become an arrow pointing towards the transcendent. Then, as objective truth began to pass away and I decided that no dogmatic theology was possible, the arrow pointing up to heaven became, as one might say, internalized. It was an inner pathway of self-transcendence, and a philosophy of the religious life. Later, when even *self*-transcendence became problematic to me, I suggested that in our post-dogmatic century it is precisely our own religious struggles that change us, propelling us along a personal track of spiritual development. Later, the movement became more of a spontaneously-created work of life-art, personal and variable, as I moved towards an aesthetics of religious existence. Finally, and most recently of all, the spiritual movement became the movement of meaning itself, endlessly spilling over sideways. 'I' – the human self – became decentred.

So the labours of twenty-odd years have changed not just my 'position', and not just 'me': more profoundly, my conception of what sort of change it is that I am undergoing has been changing. The literary project takes on a Chinese-box quality: as I change, the project changes – *and the change changes, too*.

It is no secret that my work has been very unpopular in many quarters. I must take this opportunity of thanking those kind folk who by persisting in buying my books have kept me publishable, and on the road. I fear that the latest developments in my thinking must have tried their patience sorely, but I hope they'll bear with me. And I thank Scott Cowdell for the interest he has shown in my work, and for his critical reconstruction of the path I have followed.

May 1988   Don Cupitt

Preface

My interest in Don Cupitt began in 1985 when as a third-year student in an Anglican Theological College I read his *Taking Leave of God*. The scales fell from my eyes, and when later I read Harry Williams' autobiography *Some Day I'll Find You*, I recognized more clearly the harsh sort of God of whom Cupitt had helped me to take leave. Others at the college watched his BBC series *The Sea of Faith*, but while my sympathy for his work grew (though not uncritically, by any means), I was aware that my reaction was not theirs, nor was it the 'official' one.

Cupitt is a household word for extreme theological liberalism, a name too shocking even to mention in the general synod. Introducing the Doctrine Commission's latest, quite daring statement of faith last July, the Bishop of Salisbury assured the synod that in the report's index under the letter C 'a certain well-loved luminary of the Cambridge theological faculty does not figure'.[1]

Such was not always the case, however: of Cupitt's orthodoxy in 1972, David L. Edwards in the *Church Times* confidently stated that Cupitt ' . . . is a very clever man who believes in God through Christ'.[2] Eight years later, though, in an article entitled 'Atheist Priest?', also in the *Church Times*, the same reviewer called for Cupitt to resign his priests' orders.[3] Clearly some meta-morphosis had taken place and I shall seek to explicate it in what follows.

I wish to acknowledge my thanks to Don Cupitt for writing encouragingly to me and for drawing my attention to some out-of-the-way articles. To the Revd Dr Ian Gillman and the Revd Howard Munro go my thanks for their useful comments made earlier this year when the book appeared in its original form, as an honours thesis. But I would mention in particular my supervisor Dr

Philip C. Almond, Reader in Studies in Religion at the University of Queensland, whose friendship, patience and encouragement have meant a very great deal to me.

Brisbane   Scott Cowdell
Ash Wednesday 1988

Introduction

This study is not primarily a discussion of Cupitt's most notorious belief, held at least since *Taking Leave of God* (1980), that an objectively existing God is not called for to explain, justify or empower the dynamics of Christian life, though of course we shall see how such a view arose. Rather, it is a response to a notable weakness in the relatively small quantity of published material about Cupitt to date, namely its lack of an overall perspective. Many critics appear to have read only one or two of his books. The main aim of this short book therefore is to redress this imbalance. I shall examine first the twenty or so years of work culminating in *Taking Leave of God* as 'the early Cupitt' and then the later period which brings us to the present. These more recent writings represent a new and even more radical departure, yet have attracted very little attention in print.

'The early Cupitt' will be seen to have passed through two phases. In the first of these he sought knowledge of God via the cancelling of one set of religious images and symbols by another and was more conservative than in what followed. This petered out after *The Worlds of Science and Religion* (1976), which had in part been an attempt to retain a religious cosmology. In the second phase (a trajectory beginning in *The Leap of Reason* and passing through *The Nature of Man* into his works on the historical Jesus) Cupitt relocated the transcendent entirely beyond the reach of human knowing. The capacity for self-transcending thought served him as the basis for a philosophy of spirit which he identified also in the historical Jesus, who for him was 'The Last Man'. As Jesus the prophet of eschatological urgency stood at the end of the social and religious world of his own day and pointed by irony and subversive parable to a new human reality called the kingdom of God, so for Cupitt we too must stand with Jesus at the end of what was formerly for us a stable and uncomplicated world. Then in *Taking Leave of God*, having jettisoned a dogmatic view of religious truth in the face of modern doubt, pluralism, the demands of contemporary selfhood and so on, Cupitt eventually parted with theological realism altogether, demythologizing it into a critical, Protestant and individualistic spirituality which he called 'Christian Buddhism'.

'The later Cupitt', by contrast, is less individualistic, more social and more 'up-to-date'. About dogma, morality and the 'Christ of faith' too he is somewhat more *relaxed*, in keeping with the easy, eclectic spirit of the post-modernism he is discovering. Cupitt progressively traces those currents of modern thought which view the world as man-made – as constructed wholly within the web of public discourse. He eventually arrives with the radical Parisian philosophers via his most recent book *The Long-Legged Fly* (1987) in a 'two-dimensional' world of signs: entirely linguistic, beyond any sort of realism whatever, and in which all meaning is 'incarnate'. He attempts to delineate a radical Christian humanism for such severely attenuated, post-modern conditions.

In compiling a critique of Cupitt's programme, I have grouped together such errors and inconsistencies as I have identified in a subsection of Chapter III called 'A credible programme?' Other problems are considered under the heading 'An adequate religion?' A final subsection examines some of the dispute about Cupitt's orthodoxy, and his right to remain a priest. Suffice it to say that I decide in his favour, though atheism is of course in the eyes of the beholder. Very briefly, I conclude that despite its very great appeal, Cupitt's programme and his religion leave enough unanswered questions not to rule out at least a qualified theological realism.

Biographical Sketch

The following notes have been pieced together from the complete works of Don Cupitt, and from one or two hints elsewhere. They are meant to be informative about the development of his thought, but I hope that they may also help a little to humanize this rather formidable intellectual ascetic.

Don Cupitt was born in Lancashire in 1934. He conveys little of his boyhood in his books, but does mention two incidents. He recounts how at the age of ten he stole a Chelsea bun from the baker, justifying this by the deprivations of boarding-school life in 1945. The memory of this incident was as important to him as the apples were to Augustine.[1] We are told that at his school there was a huge chapel built in the 1920s as a war memorial. Over the altar was suspended a soldier's coffin in stone matching the shape of the altar, while on the walls were names of the fallen with texts like 'Greater love hath no man . . .'. He relates how even as a boy he knew that 'Remembrance Sunday theology' with its mixture of religious and political values was horribly wrong.[2] He speaks of assimilating a vaguely deistic but very English and lay-Anglican sounding sort of religion at fourteen, only to lose hold of it. He was converted back to religion at eighteen.[3]

From a background in the long-secularized industrial north-west Cupitt came to Trinity Hall at Cambridge as an undergraduate and was very influenced by studying biology and the history and philosophy of science, graduating in 1955. He had been introduced to the thought of Karl Popper by his supervisor N. R. Hanson, who was himself inclining at that time to constructivism, teaching that all observations are theory-laden and so foreshadowing a more developed anti-realism in later philosophy of science. It was then that Cupitt took in the idea that the truth of science does not reside in any body of 'truths' but in the 'purgative way' of its zeal to falsify, affirming 'the modern intellectual virtues: doubt, scepticism, self-criticism'.[4] Thus Cupitt brought to theological study an awareness of the objections to realism: that is, to the common view that our theories (be they scientific or theological) refer to real things in the external world, and are not simply convenient and consistent 'fictions'.

The form of religion in which Cupitt was involved as an undergraduate is also instructive for understanding his subsequent development.

> Though temperamentally very religious, I have never looked for or believed in miracles, answers to prayer, particular providences or the 'supernatural' in the popular sense. Hostility to anthropomorphism was reinforced by my experience as a member, after my conversion, of a conservative and pietistic Protestant group. The curiously powerful psychological tyranny which that group exercised over its members depended upon an uncritically literal use of religious language. You had to say you 'knew the Lord', but you were not allowed to question precisely what could be *meant* by a claim to 'know' the Lord. Ever since, I have equated anthropomorphism with bondage to idols, and the negative way with spiritual freedom.[5]

Having found religious authority in this system too extrinsic and believing it to be too concerned with institutional power and authority, Cupitt proceeded while studying biology to an altogether more Protestant, moralized and internalized version of this position.[6]

Cupitt then went on to Westcott House in Cambridge in 1957, gaining a First Class in Part Three of the Theological Tripos in 1958. Under the supervision of George Woods ('I am a Cambridge Lati-tudi-narian'), he graduated painlessly from natural science into a moderate version of British empiricism and eighteenth-century moral philosophy.

In Cambridge at this time, philosophy stopped with Kant, and resumed with Moore and Russell. When Woods claimed to be unable to make anything of Kierkegaard, Cupitt was silent, having begun reading him on the side.[7] Later, he was much influenced by the projection theories of Freud, Feuerbach and Durkheim.[8] He was impressed too by the direct confessional style of Harry Williams and the 'Feuerbachian Essays' of John Wren-Lewis, but any influence was slow-burning and subliminal. He was not much influenced by the non-cognitive philosophies of religion, which were then mostly rather slight. At the time too, Cupitt knew nothing of modern French thought; the channel being wider than the Atlantic.[9]

On Trinity Sunday 1959, the year he obtained his MA, Cupitt was ordained deacon by the Bishop of Manchester, William Greer, to a curacy at St Philip's, Salford. He made his pilgrimage back to 'the strange Lancashire wasteland',[10] partly to reconnect with his origins after an education in the south-east and partly because like several friends he believed it necessary to test his understanding of Christianity against the realities of life in an industrial city[11] (Manchester and Salford being the oldest large industrial area in the world).

The radical theology of the 1960s did not affect Cupitt much at first, nor until much later did advice given him at the time to 'get up-to-date' by studying Blake and Nietzsche. Yet while he was working as an assistant chaplain at Salford Royal Hospital, his conviction began to mount nevertheless that religious beliefs are not about 'the way things are'. God was not to be found among the causes of the sickness he encountered, as The *Book of Common Prayer* would have it, but rather in the possibility of escaping the confines of a narrow consciousness attendant upon any such misfortune. Declaring himself young and foolish, Cupitt notes how he failed at the time to work out the implications of this: that God is better understood as a refuge than as a theory.[12] He was, however, coming to the view that his religious actions as chaplain were not an 'auxiliary technology' to the science-based work of the hospital but rather were to be done for their own sakes, disinterestedly. Cupitt thinks that he came closest to this view around three o'clock one morning after leaving a death bed. The patient had been alone and unconscious, and Cupitt felt certain that his giving of the last rites would in no way have altered the patient's eternal destiny from what it might otherwise have been. Yet he was glad to have turned out, and hoped that when his time came, someone might do the same for him. The religious act itself was intrinsically good, regardless of any subsequent 'pay-off', affirming human values in an otherwise vast and unfriendly universe.

We may note in passing Cupitt's evaluation of his Anglican tradition at this time, with its lively Protestant and Catholic strands and its strong sense of history. He had come to adopt the Platonic and mystical style of religion which in *Life Lines* he calls 'Ladder realism', becoming acquainted with the spiritual classics of the West (which feature prominently in his later work). In his thirties, Cupitt became somewhat involved with the historically conscious religion and attenuated form of realism which we encounter in his earlier books and articles.[13]

In 1962 Cupitt succeeded Robert Runcie and John Habgood (later Archbishops of Canterbury and York) as Vice-Principal of his old theological college. In 1966 he became Fellow and Dean of Emmanuel College, Cambridge. Cupitt was Stanton Lecturer in the Philosophy of Religion from 1968 to 1971 (the origin of his first two books, *Christ and the Hiddenness of God* and *Crisis of Moral Authority*). He was made an Assistant University Lecturer in Divinity from 1968 and Lecturer from 1973. He is still Fellow and Dean of Emmanuel, still a Lecturer in the Philosophy of Religion at Cambridge. He is married, with three children (an engaging discussion between John and Caroline, then five and four, begins his book *The Worlds of Science and Religion*).

In his preface to the second edition of *Christ and the Hiddenness of God* in 1985 Cupitt looks back over the intervening years, noting how very slowly his thinking has changed. Yet changed it has. He mentions how in *Christ and the Hiddenness of God* his instincts were still with realism, but how since 1980 he has argued in the opposite direction, having begun to see the will-to-realism (as deeply rooted in him as in everyone else) to be a profound religious mistake.

Since *Taking Leave of God*, in what I am calling his later period, Cupitt has been trying to get even more 'up-to-date' (as he often puts it), reckoning with Nietzsche (*The World to Come*), Wittgenstein (*The Sea of Faith*) and with (since *Only Human*) what Harland has called French 'superstructuralism'. This has led him to ethics and to the practical question of what is to be done. Asking himself recently just how much of his earlier work he disavows, Cupitt likens himself to an artist who shifts emphasis over time, but does not think of this in terms of progress. His views have changed since *The Leap of Reason* was written for instance, but he will not disclaim it.[14] This new-found religious tolerance is a feature of the later period, especially since *Only Human*. Summing up the shifts in his thinking in a recent interview, Cupitt put it this way:

> I started from a position of super-high orthodoxy which gradually turned into a non-objective belief in God at the end of the seventies. Since then I've moved away from Christian existentialism towards a more social, linguistic Christian humanism.[15]

To end this biographical sketch, it is perhaps useful to draw a distinction between Cupitt and another contributor to that notorious symposium *The Myth of God Incarnate* (1977), Michael Goulder. Goulder resigned his orders after announcing that he had ceased to believe in a personal God and Cupitt has been challenged to do the same. Yet while Cupitt certainly does not believe in a personal God there is no parallel in his writings to the litany of spiritual dryness we find in an essay by Goulder entitled 'The Fram Abandoned'.[16] Goulder had never known religious experience and seems to have abandoned religion for that reason. Cupitt, however, mentions two experiences of his own, albeit interpreting them as theory-laden.[17] One, of the 'extravertive type', followed upon seeing a massive wistaria in full bloom in Trinity Great Court in the summer of 1955, suggesting heaven and eternity by the arresting magnificence of its blossoms. Another, of the 'mystical type', involved his experience in the spring of 1953 of several weeks of abiding warmth and religious happiness. Interpreting it at the time as the presence of God, Cupitt nevertheless noted how extraordinarily undifferentiated it was. He concludes that although his religious experience has been (and occasionally still is) quite vivid, he cannot see any cognitive content in it. We are told that even when Cupitt was a realist, his conviction was largely philosophical.[18]

Finally, we note how self-deprecating Cupitt is throughout the autobiographical snippets, admitting that his explorations may have led him into many errors. He claims indifference about this, leaving the matter for history to decide.[19]

I

The Early Cupitt

1. First Phase

Perhaps the most notable feature of Cupitt's early work is its high monotheism. It is a religion of God rather than man, and the Kierkegaardian 'infinite qualitative distinction' between the two sets limits on human religious knowing. There is none of the 'friendly, involved God' of Eli Wiesel's famous prison-camp story, nor the 'fruity, pagan language' of Jürgen Moltmann's theology, where God suffers along with the victims of oppression.[1] According to the early Cupitt 'man-sized religion' offers no hope. The secular theology of the 1960s is his *bête noir*: having emptied God into Christ, this theology proceeds to reduce Christ to man, thus running the risk of divinizing any human system or project one wishes. Herein lie Cupitt's fears about dogma, and especially in this early period about the doctrine of the incarnation. To exalt the human too highly is to destroy belief in God,[2] and hence to limit the breaking and remaking over-againstness of transcendence in human life. For Cupitt, then, a high theism is a spiritual necessity. There is evidence of this anti-dogmatic attitude in first article from 1961, in which he denies that any one church has 'the truth' at the expense of another.[3] (This is echoed in his contribution to the Cambridge Christology symposium in 1972, where he denied any dogmatic essence of the church, describing Christianity as a family of monotheistic faiths finding in various ways in Jesus the key to the relation of man with God.)[4]

What sort of religious knowledge did Cupitt favour then? There is limited recourse to natural theology in a 1964 paper,[5] but soon afterwards Cupitt immersed himself in the regulative truths and qualified analogies of H. L. Mansel and the earlier theological 'dries' of the generation after Locke – Anglican theology's 'golden age'.

In a 1967 article, 'Mansel's Theory of Regulative Truth', Cupitt gives a sympathetic assessment of Mansel's 1858 Bampton Lectures, *The Limits of Religious Thought Examined*, and particularly his view that religious truths are not descriptive of supernatural things, but are rather regulative truths referring to the living-out of religious commitment. In replying to the philosophical unbelief of the time, Mansel (1820–1871) donned the mantle of Butler, attacking 'pernicious' German rationalism and biblical criticism. Faith accepts revelation. The realities behind it are inaccessible, yet there is enough there to live by, and any speculation or biblical criticism is idle: 'Scripture is for salvation!' Kant and Schleiermacher were particular offenders, but Mansel nevertheless held to Kant's metaphysical agnosticism and to Schleiermacher's grounding of religious belief in a feeling of absolute dependence. The resultant (carefully hedged) natural theology was unimpressed with the then current arguments from design and with doctrines of analogy involving notions of 'proportion' or 'resemblance' by which reason has direct access to 'divine things'. Philosophical theology must maintain a proper *distance* between divine things and human things. Mansel marked out Kant's moral critique of revelation, based on practical rather than pure reason, for special scorn. He saw it as a contradiction of Kant's own metaphysical agnosticism, as well as the worst excess of rationalism. Scriptural revelation provided anthropomorphic pictures of God and his will which had regulative but not descriptive value, yielding a pattern for religious obedience. Though no fundamentalist, Mansel did have a certain 'goodwill towards orthodoxy'. His aim was 'to defend the authority of revelation as a whole against the rationalists who denied its authority and also the dogmatists who mistook its character'.[6] A byword for ' . . . chilly logic and austere high-church toryism',[7] Mansel is perhaps best understood as representing the old Anglican emphasis on 'practical divinity'.

This theme of affirmation and denial as continual twin foci of religious knowing and acting is continued in Cupitt's first book, *Christ and the Hiddenness of God*. Based on the Stanton Lectures given at

Cambridge in the Lent terms of 1969 and 1970, the book approaches theistic belief from the philosophy of religion with a particular focus on christology, considering how God might be known through Christ.

In dealing with philosophical problems for belief in God, Cupitt notes the fundamental bipolarity of theism. Immanent and transcendent poles are logically built into 'God-talk', which must use anthropomorphic images and then break them. Affirming this restless, iconoclastic dimension of theism, he criticizes on the one hand the doctrines of analogy which claim direct access to God and on the other the voluntarist views which find faith self-authenticating without reference to 'fact'. Instead one must combine the traditional affirmative and negative ways, which Cupitt identifies respectively with Cleanthes and Demea from Hume's *Dialogues Concerning Natural Religion*, of 1779. Cupitt then asks if Christ can shed any light on this.

Cupitt begins by working out just what is the reference for the word 'Christ'. He rejects the Bultmannian line whereby Christ lives in the kerygma alone, actualized only through preaching. (D. M. MacKinnon calls this view 'theological occasionalism'.) He is less suspicious of the 'quest for the historical Jesus' than is Bultmann, being quite confident in the liberal manner that we can get back to the *ipsissima vox* of Jesus, and so on. Why, asks Cupitt, if the life of Jesus has no kerygmatic weight, were kerygmatic books written based on his life? He then considers whether the resurrection might be a meeting-place of fact and theology, as is often claimed. He rejects 'event theories' and 'Psi theories' (involving 'visions') in favour of 'theological theories', holding that *the Easter faith preceded the Easter events*. That is to say, the early church's reflection on the significance for it of Jesus' life against the background of its Old Testament expectations led it to resurrection faith. As a result, recognitions such as that on the road to Emmaus could have occurred, religious experiences of seeing Jesus could have been recorded and eventually empty-tomb traditions could have arisen. It is the life of the historical Jesus recorded in the New Testament which is the basis of resurrection belief and of christology more generally. Jesus is the (historical) reference for the word 'Christ'. He is not of course visible now, but Cupitt argues that we could in principle recognize and describe him and thus identify him as Jesus.

For Cupitt there is no direct analogical knowledge (*analogia entis*) of God – not even Christ can provide it. There is, however, an *analogy of proportion* based on the fact that Jesus is both the mythical and historical paradigm of what it is for people to have to do with God. The power of Jesus' proclamation was its message of the nearness of God in a world so accustomed to the opposite, while its tragedy was its portrayal of the distance of God – most clearly in the so-called 'messianic woes' and on the cross. This captures the essential bipolarity of theism.

> Christians believe that Jesus is the Christ, and still lives now, and still actively relates men to God because they discern in the narratives of his life and death the epitome of the universal human situation before God, the Yes and the No, the nearness and the farness.[8]

This 'bipolarity of theism' is a constant theme throughout Cupitt's work. For instance, in a discussion in *The Leap of Reason* of how theistic faith arises he declares the process complete when there is an 'enantiodromia' (using C. G. Jung's term) – a constant flux and reflux – between affirming the religious dogma, system, etc. on the one hand and recognizing its relativity and incompleteness before that which transcends it on the other.

> This spiritual dance is the central source of intellectual and artistic creativity in any culture. When it is lost, as it is in danger of being lost today, the sources of life are cut.[9]

Yet a shift in emphasis is about to take place. In a small but important 1970 article, 'Mansel and Maurice on our Knowledge of God', Cupitt discusses the lively debate between these two divines over the afore-mentioned 1858 Bampton lectures – a debate taking place amid a rising mood of agnosticism in England.

Mansel's point, as we have seen, was a denial of direct access to God, either by 'mystical delusions' or by rational intuition. Faith renounces such access: to know God is to do his will as set out in the regulative images provided by scripture. Maurice's approach to religious truth, like that of Newman and Matthew Arnold was ethical. He took up the moral criticism of religion begun in Kant's *Critique of Practical Reason*, seeking to reshape orthodoxy accordingly. The personal ethical knowledge making this possible was rooted in a real ontological communion between the believer and God. Despite his qualified use of Schleiermacher, Mansel had no time for such notions: the only truth or certainty available to us about God is that our images 'work' in regulating the spiritual life. In concluding, Cupitt writes:

> A few years ago it seemed to me that Mansel was nearer the truth . . . Now however, I feel a little more sympathy for Maurice's opinion, but it would be a long story to say why.[10]

Something has obviously happened, however, as Cupitt's next book is a moral critique of Christianity. The published work is rather too thin at this point for us to be certain what it was, though the continued importance of both figures for Cupitt's later work suggests more of a rapprochement than a straightforward shift of allegiance. Given that Cupitt has not surrendered Mansel's theory of regulative truth, perhaps he has come to realize that an 'idol' often comes between humanity and the God whom Mansel wishes to protect by keeping 'high and dry'. So Cupitt comes to see a distinction between the 'working God' of religion on the one hand and the ineffable transcendent on the other. Of the presence of this distinction in Cupitt's thought there is no doubt: it is a gap yawning ever wider until in *Taking Leave of God* the latter 'God' vanishes from the picture entirely. Might it be that Cupitt has realized that a 'working God', which can be seen as the subject of Maurice's attack, is not Mansel's God? To criticize the former 'God' is not to show disrespect to the latter, but is rather to dethrone an idol. This, I suggest, explains how Cupitt can come to his moral critique in *Crisis of Moral Authority*, understanding it as a purge for religion, and yet remain 'Manselish' in his theism at the same time.

Sub-titled 'The Dethronement of Christianity', *Crisis of Moral Authority* represents Cupitt's second set of Stanton Lectures – those for 1971. The title of the preface to the first edition, 'The Cleansing of the Temple', further sets the scene for what follows, in which he administers a moral purge in eight 'doses'. A church which often claims moral superiority is here reminded that those who reject its message often do so on moral grounds, and that such rejection is more serious than were, for instance, the doctrinal problems of the 1960s. Cupitt uses the criticisms of a number of freethinkers, agreeing or disagreeing as needs be in a fair assessment. His aim is renewal in the church and his goal an honest, theistic Christian humanism. Much influenced by Karl Popper's view of scientfic method, as we have seen, Cupitt locates truth not in a body of statements but in the search. In the process of unmasking idols and rejecting illusion truth is what remains.

The first 'dose' calls for the rejection of the '*old, anthropomorphic story-theology*'. The worst excesses of the cosmic redemption myth – ideas of election, fall, substitutionary atonement, theodicy, and so on – were collapsing under moral pressure in Mansel's day, but they remain in liturgy and popular imagination despite the best insights and efforts of modern theologians. The second attack is on *asceticism* and especially the traditional 'virtues' of the religious life: renunciation of property, obedience to ecclesiastical superiors, sexual abstinence and vigilance. While admitting that these notions are not wholly devoid of value if correctly applied (all but the second), he nevertheless locates their basis in essentially non-Christian ideas, such as Plato's opposition of reason and the passions, and Augustine's *ordo amoris*, by which one should love things only in proportion to their rank in the scale of being. Cupitt discerns in all of this the marks of an intropunitive religious psychology: repression, anxiety and scrupulosity. Thirdly *the subjection of women*, while not at all entailed by Christian 'theory', has often been the Christian practice. It was only with the rise of secularism and the collapse of all that underpinned an Aristotelian world-view (including the discovery last century of the female ovum and so of the woman's full biological role in conception) that the church could begin to mend its ways. Fourthly Cupitt decides that *monotheism is characteristically intolerant* (over against the usually more easy-going polytheism), and notes the important role that factions have played in Christianity from the start. However, he concedes that a firm religious line was needed for social cohesion before the appearance of the pluralistic modern state in the seventeenth century. He goes on to suggest that the days of the *Augustinian two-city theology* have gone now that the church has lost its social power. He thinks that a 'one-city theology' with a weaker ecclesiology is more suitable to the church's present situation (do we detect here more evidence of his new fondness for F. D. Maurice?). He then turns to *imagery of domination and submission*, examining Kant, Hegel and Freud with their various suggestions that the Christian view of God leaves believers with too poor a self-image. Then he considers differing opinions of the utilitarians Paley and Bentham on *the utility of religion*. Whereas Paley and many moderns would consider religion a good thing in affirming moral values, Bentham, Freud and others would not. Yet Cupitt notes how the deepest things of religion and morality come together in occasions like weddings, precisely where religion seems least able to add anything to the basic nature of the act. The criticisms of Bentham and Freud thus seem idle. Finally, in dialogue with Walter Kaufmann's book *The Faith of a Heretic* Cupitt the theologian defends his craft despite its incompleteness, fallibility, etc. But he criticizes the church as a 'doctrinal hoarder' afraid of challenge and development, advocating a more critical view. He urges it to be ' . . . less tolerant of the obscurantism and intellectual permissiveness of a good deal of church life'.[11] He mentions too the need somehow to affirm the finality of Christ while being open to the insights of other religions, again suggesting a distinction between the religious symbol and that to which it points.

Cupitt's shift to the second phase of his early period is not so much a transition as a following through of the inherent impulse of this first phase – the same shift that I suggested was involved in his synthesizing of Mansel and Maurice. A nail is already in the coffin of theological realism at this stage, in that as we have seen the God of religious programmes is not to be identified with the transcendent. Natural theology is gone and analogy, too, is unsure now that the two 'Gods' are separate. Yet some possibility of religious disclosure remains for Cupitt, as we shall see with reference to three last pieces of work.

Cupitt describes his 1975 paper 'The Meaning of Belief in God' as his last defence of the doctrines of the Trinity and the Incarnation. He was at the time writing *The Worlds of Science and Religion* and still searching for a Christian cosmology.[12]

He addresses two paradoxes of monotheistic belief. First, such religion requires an approach to the transcendent via a particular name and through a particular religious programme (many of which are really quite mutually exclusive). Monotheism therefore links the universal and cosmological with the highly particular and social. The Christian expression of this paradox in the Incarnation is of the fusing in one person of the universal *Logos* with a fully historical life. Secondly, monotheism demands a mix of order and freedom: the interplay of positive and negative ways by which a believer within the programme must nevertheless transcend the programme.

> Thus religion is concerned with cosmic order, social order and spiritual freedom, and these three concerns are one. The symbol of all this in Christianity is the doctrine of the Trinity; there is the universal creator, there is the social Body of Jesus Christ, and there is the free Spirit: and these three are one, in such a way that God can only be known as the unity of the three concerns.[13]

In a 1975 article, 'God and the Futures of Man', Cupitt is still searching for a synthesis of the spirits of science and religion: 'Its achievement would be the rebirth of faith in God, the relating of all aspects of our experience to one who is holy, all-wise, and all-good.'[14] But in *The Worlds of Science and Religion* in particular we find Cupitt's last attempts in this area.

This book in an Issues in Religious Studies series asks whether science has destroyed religion by destroying any cosmology linking the natural and moral orders. Cupitt considers the future of a society with no inherent values, and is in the end still unable to abandon a religious cosmology.

He begins with a dispute between his two children, four and five years old, over human origins. Did God make us, or are we products of the evolutionary process? Cupitt suggests that both statements are 'true', ushering in the 'two worlds' view of science and religion. That is to say, they occupy logically distinct worlds, and their assumptions are not incompatible. Cupitt notes, however, that there is no cross-cultural problem of science and religion, and that the particular issues raised for Christianity arise because its unity is not racial (for instance) but doctrinal. Christianity has depended on an enormously ambitious all-encompassing world-picture, which was so sensitive and interconnected that geographical or scientific discoveries could seriously disrupt it, as has increasingly been the case since the sixteenth century. Cupitt mentions the man-centred religious cosmos of the ancient Nile valley and the 'humanizing' of Babylonian and Sumerian myths by the Hebrews as examples of an element still present in Richard Hooker, who gave ' . . . a cosmological backing to the orderly mattins and evensong that are read in an English village church'.[15] Such views have now broken down and in their place has appeared an interventionist God (accompanied by heightened interest in 'the miraculous') or else a pietism which shifts religious attention from the outer to the inner realm.

Cupitt goes on to consider the turning of the tools of science upon man himself, referring to the growth of medicine and to the rise of statistics which by making the future a matter of probability rather than Providence have led to the institution of life assurance and similar practices. It was Darwin in particular who contributed to this new mood of religious uncertainty, as people's belief in their special status within the cosmos was eroded. Freud, too, located the basis of much human activity in the primal urges linking us to our pre-human forebears, while scholars in the new discipline of religious studies identified the roots of our religious practices in ancient non-rational sources. Here, as earlier in his response to the loss of a Christian cosmology, Cupitt suggests that Christians should make the best of all this, developing a love for the biological and the contingent within which we are bound and gladly surrendering any sense of power that our former 'importance' seemed to justify.

Cupitt then turns to the impact of science on the appreciation of ritual and symbol. For him rituals are symbolic statements and affirmations of the social order, but in practice the line between the symbolic and the practical within ritual is a fine one (as in the rituals of tea making and those of the law court). Associating the rediscovery of the importance of ritual with Lévy-Bruhl, Cupitt nevertheless denies his suggestion that all it reflects is a dreamlike, pre-modern state of consciousness, favouring instead the opinion of Evans-Pritchard that such behaviour is totally explicable as part of a complete *Gestalt*.

Cupitt recognizes the need for a public cosmology linking the moral and natural orders, and denies that science (and particularly the aggressively value-laden positivistic scientism, now thankfully on the wane) can provide it. Yet without it, the public world has no meaning and any human future is in doubt. He notes, however, that religions of redemption aspire beyond the present order, drawing from it symbols to point (albeit imperfectly) to ' . . . a perfect good that lies beyond it, and is our final home'.[16]

2. Second Phase

Cupitt's unease with a typically English synthesis of science and religion first appeared in his 1975 article 'Darwinism and English Religious Thought'. English religion had no infallible book or church. It had made much of the argument from design since the mid-seventeenth century, depending on the discernment of God's handiwork in nature. (England had after all produced that peculiar saint, the parson naturalist.) However, for Cupitt the main reason for Darwin's unpopularity was that this view broke down in response to Darwinism. He concludes the paper with a new insight, which we have just encountered perched uneasily at the end of *The Worlds of Science and Religion*: the nineteenth century had no reason to fear Darwin because in any case nature and grace were never meant to be smoothly continuous. Monotheistic religion is in part a reaction against nature, taking seriously the problem of evil. A religion of redemption can never be content with nature as it is. This view is echoed in an essay called 'Natural Evil', prepared for the same symposium. Cupitt calls for a halt to the uncritical quasi-paganism of an age obsessed with 'the natural' which lacks confidence about human beings' capacity to improve nature through their work.

> The Christian respects wild nature, but neither regards it as an end in itself, nor worships it. It is not yet perfected, but it waits for its redemption, which will come through the work of men redeemed by God in Christ.[17]

Yet as early as *The Leap of Reason*, modern relativism and pluralism had taken their toll of Cupitt's former certainties. There was no longer any clear vision of where the road strewn with broken idols might lead. Thus he came to see knowledge of God as beyond any symbolism, cosmology or world view and as possible only when one's ordered world passes away altogether in a pure act of a self-transcendence. The meaning of the historical Jesus was beginning to become clear to Cupitt as an instantiation of this principle and the book was supposed to have been a veiled interpretation of Jesus.

Instead of lamenting pluralism and relativism as modern curses and as causes of the death of God Cupitt seeks to drive home their reality and unavoidability, presenting them as valuable pointers to the transcendent. He sets about developing a phenomenology of spirit able to draw together their best features, concluding with a vindication of theism as the best and most realistic religious response, with Christianity favoured in particular.

The Leap of Reason begins with the denial of any privileged position for science in the limiting of relativism. Science itself *adds* to scepticism via anthropology and psychology and since Kuhn's book *The Structure of Scientific Revolutions* cannot claim to be value-neutral. Religious truth too is a subjective business, more moral than logical. But despite the lack of absolute reference points, Cupitt nevertheless seeks an approach that will minimize illusion. This leads to the heart of the book, where Plato's allegory of the cave is restated in an attempt to offer a more credible model of human approach to the transcendent. Instead of seeing shadows from outside the cave as in Plato's original, the modern cave-dweller has no signals of transcendence whatever. He is, however, aware of other worlds in dream, imagination, in the normal identification of sub-worlds contained within our world and interacting with it (such as the feeding of fish in a tank), in experiences of incompleteness and frustration or alternatively of hope; and in the biological drives of insatiable desire. A flash of intuition based on all of this enables an awareness of one's finitude and of the relativity of one's own position – a distancing and a self-transcendence which Cupitt (after Kierkegaard) calls 'the leap of reason'. The cave-dweller's spirituality is his capacity to make this leap, which leads to no knowledge of anything outside his world, but merely to a new perspective on it, after which it appears completely different.

For Cupitt, this is an appropriate religious perspective. Though it offers no independent standpoint for self-appraisal, it does highlight the limitedness and relativity of every position and programme. The transcendent can be seen as constitutively hidden and ineffable – the screen for endless projections. Cupitt discusses the 'interpretative plasticity of the world' by which the various programmes adopted in interpreting experience act to generate that experience. So theistic belief yields up a theistic sort of experience and the same is true in every other sphere where belief and experience feature. This sense of universal relativism is none other than the old religious insight into the transience and corruptibility of things, yet it is a transcendent perspective impervious to its own rule that the truth of all statements is only relative.

Cupitt sets out the steps by which he sees theistic faith arising. First there is 'the leap' – the bare idea of transcendence. Then follows the acceptance of a religious programme which leads in turn to confirming experiences: ' . . . a projection increasingly becomes a perception'.[18] This is enough for many. Yet once one has understood the process and recognized the superiority of the transcendent to the programme chosen, another step can follow. It involves standing loose to the religious programme and the spiritual life to which that leads. This recalls the marvellous lightness of spirit and irony of the wisdom tradition in the Old Testament, or of Jesus himself. This sort of religion does not take itself too seriously. Yet those who have reached this state cannot kick away the ladder. What follows is what Cupitt has described with the image of a 'spiritual dance'. The programme is both accepted and denied, being seen as authoritative but not absolute. In this we see a favouring of the negative over the affirmative ways in theology – of mysticism over dogma – which for Cupitt is essential if the programme is not to obscure that to which it points.

Cupitt winds up with a moral analogue to all this, suggesting that true goodness should not be seen as generated by the self but is best viewed as a free gift. That is to say, the morally serious person should avoid any suggestion that moral success is grounded in personal merit, laying credit rather at the feet of the transcendent. Just as in religion the transcendent is taken seriously despite an awareness that the back-projection of a human religious programme is all one is in fact dealing with, so too in morality a theistic view of the transcendent is a 'useful fiction'. Constructing the idea of grace from within the logic of moral discourse alone in this way, Cupitt allows limited talk of the transcendent as personal, and as the final good.

In a 1977 article, 'Man Bound and Free', Cupitt delves further into the phenomenology of spirit introduced in *The Leap of Reason*.

The distinctively human quality is the capacity for self-transcendence – the capacity to 'become spirit'. His 1979 book *The Nature of Man* is a further instalment, in which he affirms the importance of religious perspectives in limiting some of the dogmatisms of science, just as science has limited religious dogmatism. He seeks to show the inadequacy of science in explaining human nature, identifying 'spirit' as its missing factor and transcendence as its missing perspective. Here, as later in *The Sea of Faith*, Cupitt points out how a religious cosmology is no guarantee of religious seriousness, contrasting Descartes with Pascal. Descartes needed God as something of a cog in his cosmological machine, while Pascal – mocked and terrified by his 'vast eternal spaces' – made up for his obvious lack of a 'cosmic home' by the existential quality of his religion. Already we have seen some christological implications of all this. Cupitt's notion of Jesus as 'The Last Man' first appears in a 1975 BBC radio broadcast under that name, in which he rejects a call by Ninian Smart for a new religious cosmology. For Cupitt, Jesus' stance at the end of his own world was his claim to contemporaneity. Because Jesus stood lightly by the religion of his day he can become *the* prophet for our own attenuated times. Jesus' mockery of religious systems was a far better pointer to the transcendent than the 'icon-christologies' which later developed. Jesus' willingness to see his own world pass away made his standpoint the only one from which a truly universal faith might grow. It is to this central feature of Cupitt's second phase that we now turn.

The historical Jesus and Cupitt's Christ

For C. G. Jung, Christ was best understood as archetype of the self, while for Paul Tillich he was the 'new being'. For both, as for many others, it seems that the Christ was primarily a principle rather than a person. Cupitt had always made much of the historical Jesus, though we will see his certainties in this area deteriorate in the later 1970s. Yet Jesus had also been the instantiation of a principle for him, hence the reference in the title of this sub-section to 'Cupitt's Christ'.

We have seen that in *Christ and the Hiddenness of God*, as well as being quite sure about the historical accessibility of Jesus, Cupitt also saw in him the paradigmatic picture of human relationship with

God. In his 1972 article 'One Jesus, Many Christs', he sees in the abundance of Christ images (biblical, literary, cultural, etc.) various images of perfection or of divine-human harmony.[19]

To Cupitt in the second phase of his early period Jesus comes to instantiate another principle – Cupitt's new view of 'spirit'. His first specific public airing of the new christology was a mid-1976 article (in fact a television script) printed in the BBC magazine *The Listener*. Entitled 'The Original Jesus', this article fills out Cupitt's views in 'The Last Man'. He presents Jesus as a sort of Jewish Socrates, evoking God in an indirect and ironic way which would be quite familiar to Jews.

> His sense of an enveloping conflict of good and evil was so strong that he in effect lived at the end of the world, in the presence of the ultimate realities of human life . . . because he lived at the end of time, he is for all time.[20]

With the BBC producer Peter Armstrong Cupitt produced in 1977 the book of his first foray into major broadcasting, *Who Was Jesus?*. With tremendous historical assurance, the main aspects of Jesus' life and ministry are set out. In a thoroughly liberal manner we are encouraged to seek out the historical Jesus beneath the kerygmatic accretions in which the church has hidden his message. By the time his article in *The Myth of God Incarnate* appeared, Cupitt had obviously warmed to the project in which he had shown no interest five years earlier in 'One Jesus, Many Christs' – that of using the historical Jesus to cut back the church's various 'Christs'. In this paper, 'The Christ of Christendom', Cupitt points out how the subtlety and irony that he finds in the historical Jesus is flattened out by orthodox christology, which mutes the disjunction between God and man that for him is alone salvific. He suggests that Jesus should be allowed to be used as a criticism of developed Christianity, just as the teachings of the original Buddha might call the later and more developed teachings of Mahayana Buddhism into question. Cupitt's attack on the doctrine of the Incarnation continues from various perspectives, suggesting particularly that it represents a deterioration of New Testament faith. Yet at the same time, we witness the decline of his strong liberal faith in the capacity to reconstruct Jesus' historical life, *ipsissima vox* and so on. In his article 'Jesus and the

Meaning of God' which appeared in the 1978 symposium *Incarnation and Myth*, Cupitt moves his emphasis from the words of Jesus to his distinctive 'voice'. So it is that in his 1979 book *The Debate about Christ*, he can speak of how Jesus' voice conveys the voice of God; of how Jesus is God's word or call to humankind incarnate.[21] In *Jesus and the Gospel of God* which appeared earlier in the same year Cupitt previewed this theme by looking to 'Jesus the teacher' not in terms of what he did or of the content of his now increasingly uncertain message but rather in terms of the *form* of his teaching. Cupitt drew on a variety of New Testament scholars to highlight the manner of Jesus' proclamation, involving the indirect revealing of the Kingdom of God in parables and other sayings by the use of such linguistic devices as the 'divine passive', 'antithetical parallelism' and so forth.

These developments reveal Cupitt's realization that he had assumed too much and had to recant. He mentioned in a 1982 dialogue with John A. T. Robinson how since his conservatism in this area began to give way in 1975 he had been brought up to date by friends.[22] Elsewhere he writes:

> I took what might be called a historical realist view of Jesus, in the traditional liberal manner, and have only retreated from it very reluctantly. In particular I clung to his end-of-the-world apocalypticism and to what I believed to be his *ipsissima vox* in the parables and reversal-sayings, building a good deal on them in a way that made it all the harder to surrender them.[23]

Critical Christian ethics

Moral philosophy has been a continual preoccupation of Cupitt's and the shift to the second phase of his thought in this early period also led to a new understanding of Christian ethics. He never reduces the religious to the moral in the manner of Kant or of such non-cognitivists as R. B. Braithwaite. In two articles written in 1967 but published much later Cupitt explains the link between religion and morality.[24] It is not a formal link, but religion acts as would any culture to influence the sort of moral decisions which will be made within it. In a 1975 article originally appended to the first edition of *The Leap of Reason*, 'Christian Existence in a Pluralistic Society', Cupitt points out how moral certainties have collapsed with the result that the concept of the 'ordinary upright individual' is now problematic. How then should a Christian act? Cupitt illustrates three alternatives: the bourgeois ethic of 'supplementing' the world; Kierkegaard's 'transforming' approach; or a radical alternative life-style such as that of St Francis or even of Tolstoy. A 1976 paper 'Christian Ethics Today' laments that this lack of certainty seems to have stifled the capacity of churches to speak with any force on moral issues in the contemporary situation. Afraid of modernity and hampered, according to Cupitt, by the impact of biblical theology with its 'canonizing of the past' the churches are impotent moral leaders, trailing belatedly behind the freethinkers.

Yet by 1978 in his article 'Critical Christian Ethics'[25] Cupitt's new critical philosophy of spirit was beginning to affect his ethical thinking, allowing him to find the contemporaneity he called for in the 1976 paper. Cupitt attempted to relate various Christian ethics to the kingdom ethic of Jesus as he was coming to understand him. While the *formal nature of the moral* (the good, 'ought', etc.) is still seen to be grounded in the way things are (in the spirit of the first phase of this early period), the *form of the moral* has become that critical principle which Cupitt has been espousing. The critical, apocalyptic insight of Jesus always brings things up-to-date. As we have seen before with Cupitt, to be the follower of Jesus is to be his contemporary at the end of the world.

In the next eighteen months separating this article from 'The Ethics of this World and the Ethics of the World to Come' Cupitt makes a further shift to the 'left' symptomatic of the realization in his second phase that religious knowledge cannot be grounded in the way things are.[26] So human nature, the natural order, and so on have ceased to be the ground of the formal nature of the moral. In supporting this view Cupitt draws attention to the problems of delineating any cross-cultural morality: they are as formidable as those involved in finding a cross-cultural religion. Far better, says Cupitt, to abandon any search for solid evidence upon which to base moral thinking and turn to the perspective of the last man. The essence of Christian morality is not to be found in any teaching or world view but in the critique of all teachings and all world views.

This is quite contrary to what we might call a 'moral majority view' of Christian ethics, by which I mean a set of 'Christian moral principles', 'family values' and whatever other home-grown items one wishes to bring forward for baptism. Cupitt would not reject such things out of hand, but neither would he seek the essence of Christian morality in these 'rules'. He would seek it, rather, in the subjection of all such 'morality' to rigorous examination in the spirit of the last man. He now finds this the only acceptable way of linking morality to God which he now believes to provide a perspective for constant moral remaking. This he finds illustrated by the parables of Jesus where the normal moral reasoning of the day, with all its attendant virtues of prudence and common sense in train, was subjected to the most rigorous assault and overturned. One can hardly imagine telling the moral majority that prostitutes may well enter the kingdom of heaven before them, but this is just what Cupitt might do. The forces of self-righteousness and inertia identified in *Crisis of Moral Authority* as stifling morality might then be subdued, thus enabling Christian action to become a far more 'liberating praxis'. The strident proponents of 'Christian Morality' might then hear the voice of the last man (perhaps for the first time!) and be brought to heel. Cupitt's next book, *The New Christian Ethics*, to be published in 1988, will develop this theme further in the light of the features of his later period which we have yet to examine in detail.

3. Taking Leave of God

We must now devote some attention to Cupitt's most controversial book, which he describes as the completion of a phase in this thinking starting from *Christ and the Hiddenness of God* and before and as preceding the 'conversion' leading to *The World to Come* and hence to the remainder of his later works.[27] Cupitt does in fact point out some hints of his more developed view in earlier writings.[28] Now, however, he has struggled free of his former theological realism.

Taking Leave of God is a brisk forced march along the negative way intended to induce a purge of Christianity's ingrained eudae-monism.[29] It begins and ends as a moral critique of developed Christian faith, seen here as a heteronomous external control system. It focusses on three themes in the response of religion to modern secularism: the internalization of religious meaning which has followed the enlightenment; the post-Renaissance theme of autonomy (indeed, the original title of the book was to have been *The Autonomy of Religion*);[30] and the biblical hope of a new covenant, with the law written upon the heart.

The book is very Kantian. It features a Kantian agnosticism about the existence of God whereby he cannot be inferred from experience (in this case room is left for the possible existence of an unknowable transcendent, but not for any objective, knowable God). Disinterestedness, too, is in abundance here, being perhaps the key element in Kant's understanding of ethics. We meet also the Kantian notion of the will as creator of value, which for Cupitt means that we ourselves must fill the gap created by the collapse of older moral certainties.[31]

Summing up the main points, we have: 1. The objective existence of God is in doubt theologically. 2. Such a God is of no further religious use anyway, being part of a harmful religious psychology of external authority (again, very Kantian). 3. But we are subject to a religious requirement, which is the highest spiritual principle. 4. God is the religious concern reified; the demands and promises of spirituality in coded form (like the Dharma and Nirvana in Buddhism). 5. Speculation about any extra-religious existence of God is religiously vulgar and immature. 6. It is spiritually important to attend to the present life, and not seek any hereafter.

Cupitt calls his view a 'qualified form of Theism'.[32] Much of traditional Christian faith and practice is demythologized into an individualistic spirituality; partly, one suspects, so that it can be kept on. So for instance worship, personal prayer and intercession survive, as do mythical notions such as Eden, Heaven and even God; the latter as a valuable 'as if'. But we are warned against the dangers of gratuitous over-belief, though theistic language and practice is allowed if handled cautiously. Myth and narrative are seen as indispensable for talking about the transcendent, and traditional religious materials are affirmed as often being of splendid and unsurpassed quality.[33] So worship, for instance, becomes the declaration and enactment of one's commitment to religious values – Christian belief is this commitment, and the Christian experience of God is the experience of the impact of these values in the life of faith.[34]

Western academic interest in Buddhism has recently moved out of Oriental and religious studies departments into the substantive concerns of philosophy and theology. Two recent English examples have been Derek Parfit's ground-breaking contribution to moral philosophy, *Reasons and Persons* (1984), and Ninian Smart's Gifford Lectures of 1979/80, *Beyond Ideology*. Cupitt adds to this trend with *Taking Leave of God*, attracting much comment about his 'Christian Buddhism'. The possible workability of the notion will be considered in Chapter III; for now it is enough to note that Cupitt does not embrace Buddhism *tout court*: 'The content, the spirituality and the values are Christian, the form is Buddhist'.[35]

> His selflessness, for instance, is a traditional Christian mystical self-naughting or self-emptying rather than a Buddhist onto-logical selflessness. That is to say, it is a spiritual strategy rather than a metaphysic; an instrument of the self's salvation rather than a description of what that salvation is.[36]

For Rowan Williams, Cupitt's point here is that what belongs to the realm of interacting egos is not to be projected on to our religious language. Cupitt therefore seeks to ensure that the central insight of the Buddhist tradition is not forgotten by Christians; that neither God nor the self is to be the subject of delighted, narcissistic probings.

> Religious practice claims to offer liberation: but if God is conceived as just another bundle of stimuli for the greedy self, and if our relationship with God takes on the . . . character of a personal love affair (longings and raptures, rows and recon-ciliations), how on earth can it liberate?[37]

As Cupitt's later period comes into view, however, and in particular its extension of this critique of theological realism to all forms of realism, then the passing away of the world we meet there *will* be seen to include some Buddhist metaphysics, and not just the Buddhist spirituality we here see emerging.

Concluding this examination of the book, let us very briefly return to the theme of Kantian agnosticism mentioned earlier, and to the possibility mentioned then of a hidden ineffable transcendent beyond existence. In a response to some letters to the editor of a journal a year later, Cupitt actually states that 'My account *has a hidden transcendent beyond objectivity* [italics mine], but no objective metaphysical world-ruling individual God'.[38] This is a great surprise, and undeniably redolent of Paul Tillich's 'God behind God', encountered in Volume 1 of his *Systematic Theology*.

4. Ancillary Issues

Liberalism

One feature of Cupitt's early period is his unresolved attitude to liberalism – theology which while beyond conservative notions of God as 'a real definable objective part of a supernatural realm', etc., conceives of God in a way equally untenable to the later Cupitt, as the immanent ground of some vague optimism about the future of the world and mankind. It sees a movement in history towards the fuller realization of creation's potential, being the sort of view we might today associate with Maurice Wiles, John Macquarrie, or Hans Küng. There are two main enclaves of liberalism in Cupitt's early period, both of which have already been mentioned in passing. The first is located in the articles prepared for the 1975 symposium *Man and Nature*, edited by Hugh Montefiore. 'Natural Evil' has God working through man's work to build a better future (cf., for instance, Maurice Wiles' 1986 Bampton Lectures, *God's Action in the World*), while 'God and the Futures of Man' features the distinctly liberal hope of the realization of the kingdom in history. However, in an article for *The Listener* magazine in 1976 Cupitt vehemently denies any identification of the Kingdom of God with social progress (and so confuses the issue somewhat).[39]

The second major enclave of liberalism was Cupitt's stance alongside Harnack and other liberal Protestant 'questers after the historical Jesus' of the late nineteenth century seeing, as it were, 'their own faces peering back at them from the bottom of the well of history'. As we have seen, Cupitt's preference for the historical Jesus over the developed Christ of faith has mellowed since 1977 (and the latter was to find even more favour in Cupitt's most recent writings).

Theological realism

As a related subject, we now consider the decline of Cupitt's realist views over twenty years or so, culminating in *Taking Leave of God*. We have heard Cupitt's claim never to have believed in miracles etc., yet he still declared his belief in God and in life after death well into the late 1970s. His early papers are very orthodox – including, for instance, an explicit declaration of belief in God and in creation in a 1961 article.[40] Looking back on a 1964 article, Cupitt describes himself as one of the hyper-orthodox young men who these days rise up to criticize him.[41] There is talk of grace and of the covenant as real things in a 1967 article,[42] and we have met David L. Edwards' assertion of Cupitt's orthodoxy in his comments about *Christ and the Hiddenness of God*, from the late 1960s.

Two articles from the 1970s point up Cupitt's increasingly tenuous hold on belief in life after death. Already in 1972, in 'The Language of Eschatology: F. D. Maurice's Treatment of Heaven and Hell', Cupitt was agnostic about what such a life will entail, though he was not then prepared to go as far as D. Z. Phillips and abandon the idea altogether. In 1976, with 'Where is Heaven Now?', the belief remained despite attempts to demythologize it into talk of a 'dying life'. All Cupitt was prepared to say about it was that he felt it to be guaranteed by the taste of 'post-mortem existence' he had already had (a definite lapse from normal epistemological rigour!).

Another example of lingering realism is a view of the Spirit as real in 'The Charismatic Illusion' of 1976. Yet in 1977, there are 'two spirits' to match Cupitt's two Gods (the one of religious symbol and the ineffable transcendent), as in talk of man's destiny being the communion of spirit (small 's') with Spirit (big 'S') beyond the world in the article 'Man Bound and Free'.

There is an interesting late survival of realism in *The Debate about Christ* from 1979, by which time Cupitt's search for pure transcendence uncontaminated by wishful thinking had moved from Jesus' flesh to his words, and to an exceedingly high-and-dry theism.

> But if an ascetical and wholly dehumanized religion is indeed empty, then surely the projection theory advanced by Feuerbach, Marx, Freud, Durkheim and others is right? Whereas if I can show that a dehumanized religion still works and is real, then I can exorcise these formidable spectres.[43]

In other words, if religion is to be seen as no more than the projection of human needs, values and so on, as these 'masters of suspicion' suggest, then Cupitt's dehumanized religion must fail. Here we see something of a last attempt to avert this outcome while yet holding to the existence of God. In *Taking Leave of God* the emphasis on dehumanized religion continues, but belief in God has come to mean something quite different, as we have seen.

Despite the uncertain status of the ineffable transcendent *vis à vis* the 'working God' of religion, it would seem that by the end of this early period Cupitt has largely surrendered theological realism.

The finality of Christ

It is not at all obvious that Cupitt should take the view he does of the significance of Jesus. John Hick, an altogether more 'orthodox' writer (at least as far as the existence of God is concerned), is happy to adopt a far 'lower view' of Jesus among the religious teachers of the world than is Cupitt. In 'The Finality of Christ' (1975) Cupitt identifies Jesus' irony and religious iconoclasm as the basis for his finality – there is no superseding the themes to which he bore witness. In a 1975 article 'The Leap of Reason' (appended originally to the first edition of the book of the same name) Cupitt asserts that Christianity embodies in its central myths the philosophy of spirit towards which Jesus was working far better than any other religion. Jesus' finality lies not as much in the content of his message as in its accessibility to everyone (rather than to some spiritual élite), and on that no more need be said. *Who Was Jesus?* is even more effusive, displaying a marked devotional tone:

> The message is final: nothing more can be said in language. And because Jesus grasped and lived it, he is rightly called saviour, mediator, redeemer, not because of what he is in himself, but because he was so possessed by that to which he bore witness. In that sense he is rightly called the absolute in time, the one who shows the way to the perfect world.[44]

This is quite a high christology, though it is functional. It is echoed in a response to Graham Stanton in the 1979 symposium *Incarnation and Myth*:

> But if I have found salvation through Jesus' voice and person, I can quite intelligibly speak of him as the human ultimate and the

crown of creation; the man who, by mirroring God, shows what the world is meant to be.[45]

In *Jesus and the Gospel of God* from the same year Cupitt also exalts ' . . . Jesus as high as possible without compromising monotheism'.[46] He notes how other religions capture the same realities as those to which Jesus pointed, mentioning Amida (Pure Land) Buddhism and some forms of Hinduism. But with critical reservations the full panoply of traditional christological titles is still allowable.

> Jesus can be called the final cause of creation in the sense that in him the highest goal is attained and the world comes to fruition, and he can be called the first-born of all creation in the sense that in him the creature at last enters into its perfect relation to the Creator and the Creator's work is complete . . . He anticipated – seized in advance – the end of all things. In that strictly eschatological sense he may be called divine.[47]

The church

Cupitt says relatively little about the church, and it would be safe to say that he took leave of ecclesiology long before he took leave of God. In his first published article, 'What do we mean by "the Church"?' (1961), he rejects the 'branch theory' which limits the church catholic to Roman, Eastern Orthodox and Anglican branches. The true church is rather to be seen as an eschatological reality, to which all the present churches point.[48] In *Christ and the Hiddenness of God* a 'one-city theology' with a weak ecclesiology is advocated. Cupitt here realizes that in its present limited form the earthly church is no 'heavenly city' and should give up any such pretensions, taking its proper place among the rest of humanity (this is very strongly redolent of the ecclesiology of F. D. Maurice). A view appears in Cupitt's 1974 paper 'Christian Existence in a Pluralist Society' that the church serves best as a sort of 'breeding station' for new life-style options.[49] A rare favourable view of the church, and one of only a very few mentions by Cupitt of the sacraments, appears towards the end of *Jesus and the Gospel of God*, the latter being described as a means for publicly and regularly enacting Jesus' 'victory'.

Given Cupitt's new critical philosophy of spirit it comes as no surprise that he has no sympathy for a church/state alliance, holy wars and for what we have heard him call 'Remembrance Sunday Theology'. The result of smudging religion and politics together is tyranny, and the death of the human spirit.[50] Cupitt joins to this a contempt for Rome and its pretensions to theological infallibility, especially with regard to the Küng and Schillebeeckx cases. Writing in *The Times Literary Supplement*, he noted how the present Pope had written a book called *The Acting Person*, advocating a dialectic of loyalty and dissidence in the relations of an individual with society. But what was good for Poland obviously was not good for Rome![51]

Finally, we note comments made in a similar vein over the Bishop David Jenkins affair in England. For Cupitt the condemnation of the Bishop's only very mildly liberal views was the replay of so many similar controversies in the history of the English church, and indeed almost identical to the furore accompanying the accession of Hensley Henson to the see of Hereford in 1919. The neo-conservatives responsible receive a severe tongue-lashing for confusing the truth of the Gospel with political power . . .

> They are Hobbesians: religion is an irrational dread of power and mystery, and the truest church is the one that is most uninhibitedly grand, rigid, and crushing. Seeing religion in these terms, they have no time for professors. They seek emotional domination and not intellectual illumination: they want to lick God's jackboots.[52]

II

The Later Cupitt

The later period is more thematically unified, more 'linear' and hence easier to treat. With only five books and few articles, there is not quite the task of weaving and unravelling just completed in Chapter I. Cupitt delves further into the pluralism he has courted for its spiritual advantages since *The Leap of Reason*, and enters the strange, unfamiliar culture and thought-world of post-modernism. He admits that *Taking Leave of God* was very much caught up in the religious disputes of the 1840s, too Kantian, and therefore in a strange way 'old-fashioned'.[1] Thus he enters upon the programme mentioned in the biographical sketch, of getting 'up-to-date'.

1. Some Themes

The world of the later Cupitt is very much more a *public world* than before. There is altogether less individualism, and we even find the denial of the basis of phase two from the early period, in that hyperbolical doubt and scepticism are no longer a way to the transcendent.[2] *The World to Come* is a shift to more social concerns after *Taking Leave of God*. *Only Human* denies any definable essence of the human, declaring the end of theological anthropology. Whatever self-understanding man has must now be found within the public, 'sociological' realm. From a beginning with his treatment of Wittgenstein in *The Sea of Faith*, Cupitt then develops through *Only Human* a view in which language constructs reality. So the later period is public in more than one way, but especially in the far reaches of the most recent books, where human communication becomes the sole 'reality'.

The world of the later Cupitt is also characterized by what we might liken to Nietzsche's *joyful wisdom*. This later Cupitt is far more relaxed and far less dogmatic, allowing his thought to develop in more world-affirming directions. *Only Human* presents a range of religious options with none of the scorn accompanying the appearance of some of them in the early period. We note too the shift in fortunes of the Christ which accompanies this. The more relaxed later Cupitt, increasingly happy with the world and its possibilities, warms to the notion of incarnation (especially since his close involvement with the historical Jesus is now almost ten years in the past).[3] This is entirely the case in *The Long-Legged Fly*, but also earlier in *The World to Come*, where the exalted Christ is no longer the gratuitous and pestilential over-belief of the early period, but is allowed to represent Cupitt's vision of 'the world to come'.

As regards *the future of Christianity*, Cupitt uses the metaphor of the sea of faith from Matthew Arnold's poem 'Dover Beach' to illustrate how Christianity, having ebbed with the tide, will then *return*; though it will not of course be the same.[4] Even in *The Long-Legged Fly*, his most recent and radical book, after years of courting the so-called 'anti-philosophers' with their views inimical to much of the mainstream of Western thought after Plato, Cupitt remains confident for the future survival of Christianity. He describes it as being like the amoeba: 'immortal', well able to ingest its own death and thus to draw life from its dissolution. One realizes, however, that such arduous images are no comfort for those who seek the quiet life theologically, preferring the 'green pastures' to the 'steep and rugged pathway'.

However, we see that Cupitt is *not entirely happy with post-modernism*. The modern period of the tragically serious existentialists is allegedly over. Post-modernism comes at the end of so much historical, cultural and intellectual innovation that there is a sense in which we have 'seen it all'. There is a danger, which Cupitt feels, that the post-modern world will therefore rest on its laurels and cease striving for meaning. So post-modern architecture will range eclectically over all previous styles, post-modern writing will

content itself with deconstructive commentaries on the literary glories of the past, and post-modern audiences will laugh at the seriousness of the modern period, caricatured by Woody Allen or Monty Python. In *Life Lines* and *The Long-Legged Fly*, Cupitt still believes that meaning is to be found and created. Though his new-found theological tolerance has that distinctive post-modern 'feel', nevertheless he is not totally at home. Despite relaxing in mid-life, Cupitt is still very serious.

Finally, brief mention should be made of three other themes. The later Cupitt is somewhat less sceptical about *the goodness of man*. In *The World to Come* in fact, he is quite convinced that the kingdom dwells incognito in the hearts of good men everywhere, needing only the stimulus of religion to be activated. There are echoes of this in his chapter 'Prometheus Unbound' in *The Sea of Faith*. And Cupitt has a new way of determining religious truth, with *an aesthetic view of good and bad religion*.[5] (There is a strong similarity here to J. L. Houlden's talk of the theologically educated as a 'religious connoisseur' in his 1986 book *Connections*.) Finally, *metaphysics survives* in the later period, but in a much attenuated form. With Buddhism, Cupitt's updated critical philosophy keeps just enough metaphysics for ' . . . clinging to the void, and practising compassion'.[6]

2. The Later Period Evolves, 1982–1987

Cupitt in 1982: *The World to Come*

In his review, John A. T. Robinson noted that while the influence of Kierkegaard from *Taking Leave of God* remains, the Kantian rationalism of the former work has been overtaken by Nietzsche. It prescribes a faith for rarefied living on the other side of the nihil, on a diet of four guiding principles: truth, disinterestedness, creativity and love. These are personified by God, while Jesus embodies and teaches them.[7] Cupitt himself claims that the book reflects recent writings of the American philosopher Richard Rorty on the French deconstructionist philosopher Jacques Derrida, is post-Nietzschean and represents a thoroughly new departure. His declared aim is to attempt to Christianize modern nihilism – to wrestle it back from

Nietzsche so that it can be experienced, as it were, as Holy Saturday. There is no dependence on nature or the emotions; all that remains is the creative choice to get out of the void.[8]

In an illuminating metaphor, Cupitt likens his position not to that of an anthropologist living among a primitive tribe, but rather to that of a Western-educated tribesman living with his people, warning them of the Western onslaught that will inevitably destroy their world, and seeking to save what he can. This highlights his appreciation of the democratic strain in Christianity, which means that aloof occupation of the high ground by the theologically illuminated simply will not do. So Cupitt is no advocate of the practice common among the theologically literate of preaching one thing and believing another. All must confront the challenge of 'Hyperborean faith'. (The Hyperboreans of Greek legend, resurrected by Nietzsche, found a warm and sustaining environment in the Arctic expanses beyond Boreas the north wind, and so must we in the environment of modern scepticism.)

Cupitt identifies three theological types: the 'conservative' (religious statements refer to a supernatural realm), the 'liberal' (a woolly cosmic optimism) and the 'radical' (the stuff of the spirit, preserving religion as an internal reality against the collapse of objective reality). The clowns and madmen in the works of Kierkegaard and Nietzsche, along with Ezekiel and Jesus, are such radical figures. They proclaimed a message that could not be understood, simply because it transcended the normal intellectual and religious categories. Announcing in various ways the end of the world, the 'radical' rejects the identification of shallow comfort and illusory assurances with true pastoral care. The appropriate virtue, then, is disinterestedness, by which the nihil is faced in all its capacity to terrify, not by erecting dogmatic bulwarks against doubt but by denying that in the self which it terrifies.

Cupitt, guiding us through these fires of modern nihilism to the new life possible on the other side, goes beyond Nietzsche, for whom the will-to-power remains – on the other side of the nihil, as everywhere – as the only metaphysical basis for a moral order. No doubt influenced by Foucault's critique of power structures, he gives up even the will-to-power. So Cupitt leads the way into the 'passive nihilism' which frightened even Nietzsche.

When the self and the world become completely deconstructed, egoism is uprooted. Only pure, undifferentiated and objectless awareness remains: the ego has lost internal structure. There is no longer anything *there* that is anxious for itself or that might attempt to assert itself by domination or by projecting and imposing its own ordered self-expression upon the world.[9]

The only way forward is along the purgative, disinterested and non-egoistic path of critical thinking: 'That alone is truth, and everything else is the product of power, fashion, custom, and choice.'[10] The old supernatural religion of (say) C. S. Lewis is gone for ever, and many Christians seem now called to dwell with the Hyperboreans on the high ground. In Hinduism, a separation of the religion of the masses from that of the enlightened is accepted, but the fundamental democratic strain in Christianity cannot accept any such distinction. Many need this bracing air of high theological altitudes, yet at the same time of course they also need the life-support systems of religion to survive (this is an assertion of Cupitt's which is obviously questionable). The simple truth of the un-knowability of God (there is more of the possibly Tillichian 'God behind God' here) forces the maturing spiritual life to ascend through the images of God. So beginning with (crudely) physical images of God and moving through social to personal images, one arrives with John of the Cross, Cupitt and others at the high ground, using the anti-images of the mystics. On the way, the nerve of selfishness, insecurity and fear of the void has been cut, freeing the Hyperborean uniquely for a socially active faith.

There is also a solid dose of Nietzschean *amor fati* in all of this, condemning as we have seen a religion of grace perfecting nature. The wild/tame distinction thrust by religion on 'unregenerate man' is questioned, so that Cupitt is able to find good in humankind. Thus while denying liberal or Marxist historical optimism, he is still able to locate a slim range of possible disinterestedness – as in his example of the blood donor. By applying the religion of Jesus as the necessary impetus and encouragement, Cupitt thinks it might be possible to drive us through the nihil to the new world (like the overactive sheepdog in Hardy's *Far From the Madding Crowd*).

Via Foucault, therefore, the formerly more Kierkegaardian and individualist Cupitt seems to have developed a social conscience. As for the Kingdom of God, he sees it both as a guiding ideal (as in earlier writings) and now as an historical possibility as well. Yet we note that he has denied all utopianism as a seedbed of tyranny. This, along with his condemnation of any religious validation of the social order and a qualified affirmation of authentic possibilities for disinterestedness, is identified with the programme of Jesus. Through Jesus' relation to the Judaism of his day, his prophecy and his death

> we can find in condensed form a relevant diagnosis, and a still-unfulfilled possibility of a new world. Perhaps we may find that people at large do after all have capacities for spiritual freedom, for disinterestedness and for altruism which the old ideologies denied them. Perhaps the new world is not 'impossible', as it has been called, but is practically necessary and close at hand.[11]

In an extempore dialogue with John A. T. Robinson in Great St Mary's, Cambridge, in 1982, Cupitt expressed his aims in the book as follows:

> If I could summarize the view I have come to in one sentence, it might go something like this: all the worlds that human beings have inhabited are now understood to be human social constructions; Christian faith is a corporate commitment to attempt to bring into being the new world proclaimed by the earthly Jesus and symbolized by the exalted Jesus Christ.[12]

Cupitt in 1984: *The Sea of Faith*

In this delightful volume Cupitt records in print and yet surpasses his second foray into major broadcasting: the BBC television series of the same name. The post-Enlightenment challenges to orthodox Christianity are presented through critical sketches of various individuals, often with entertaining biographical notes and anecdotes. The heroes of the story are Pascal, Freud, Jung, Schweitzer, Marx, Kierkegaard, Schopenhauer, Nietzsche and Wittgenstein. Cupitt later claims that this is the first survey of modern Christian thought in which the debate between theological realism and non-realism is central.

We are led to examine the rise of a mechanical view of the universe and the decline of a religious cosmology, encountering the discussion about Descartes and Pascal on religious seriousness which we met earlier. The impact of science on the modern consciousness is considered in a discussion expanded in the next book, *Only Human*. The advent of biblical criticism follows, focussing on D. F. Strauss, but especially on the tragic liberalism of Albert Schweitzer, who strove in vain alongside another failed eschatological prophet to humanize brute nature, turning the will-to-live into the will-to-*love*. Cupitt then reviews the key figures of nineteenth-century thought, passing from Kantian agnosticism to Hegel's idealism, and then following Marx and Kierkegaard on their divergent paths. He considers the impact of religious pluralism on Western religious thought, taking Arthur Schopenhauer, Annie Besant and Swami Vivekananda as examples. Cupitt urges Christianity to confront other religions without explaining them away:

So Christians will have to say 'We find salvation this way, and we think it is a way open to everyone, and in that sense we still say Jesus is the saviour of the world. Yet we must admit that there seem to be other ways to salvation that also work.' (177)

He then considers the end of the glorified public world after Napoleon and Hegel. A new privatized bourgeois world expresses itself in the interiority of much modern art, but not in the churches.

To the churches at large modernity proper, that strange new condition that first appeared in the last generation or so before 1914, remains unexplored territory, forbidding and desolate, barely habitable. (187)

The end of Aristotle (with Frege), Euclid (with Gödel, etc.) and Newton (with Einstein) replaced a stable cosmos with a meaningless flux. In such a world religion must be that advocated by Cupitt: fully voluntary, creative and courageous. So the first modernist philosopher Cupitt considers is Nietzsche and his denial of any religion or idealism which leads to hatred of the self and of life. He advocates an acceptance of the self and things as they are – 'the love of necessity,' *amor fati*. The most demanding test of one's acceptance of life is that of 'eternal recurrence': would one be able to rejoice at the possibility

of living the same life over again *ad infinitum*? Next in line is the later
Wittgenstein (of the *Philosophical Investigations*, rather than the
earlier *Tractatus*) with his view of the meaning of language being
knowable only through its use. He held to linguistic naturalism (that
there are only linguistic facts), voluntarism (that language creates the
world) and radical humanism (denying access to any reality beyond
the scope of human knowing). So where 'being' had been the main
concept for Plato and 'knowledge' for Descartes, for Wittgenstein it
was 'meaning'. The religious views which result are only just being
pieced together from Wittgenstein's unpublished notes, but they
teeter close to secular humanism, showing at the same time a
dissatisfaction with voluntarism through tinges of conservative
nostalgia and melancholy.

Cupitt denies that his argument has depended wholly on the
thought of cognitive deviants. If he had chosen 'orthodox' modern
theologians such as Barth, Bultmann, Tillich, Rahner and Pannenberg, a wide diversity disruptive of traditional realism would still
have been evident in this age of the 'artist-theologian'. He declares
the end of ' . . . the Babylonian captivity of realism', advancing his
own critical approach as an alternative. So religion is about the
present, eschewing any yearning for the beyond: it culminates in a
'joyful wisdom'. Religious disagreements are no longer about what is
objectively the case, but rather about what constitutes the best view
of the human condition. (One might add that this is no guarantee of
religious peace!) Anselm's God, seen as the ideal of perfection, will
serve the voluntarist well.

> Through human creativity guided by the Christian religious ideal
> the world is to be wholly humanized, and all Nature turned into
> art. Thus at last the world becomes . . . a divine Creation. (268)

Cupitt asserts too that an objectified God is more likely to be the
Devil.

> God (and this is a definition) is the sum of our values, representing
> to us their ideal unity, their claims upon us, and their creative
> power . . . God is man-made only in the non-startling sense that
> everything is. That is modern anthropocentrism. But even on my

account God is as real for us as everything else can be, and more primally authoritative than anything else is (269, 271).

Presenting his view that voluntarist and often tragic religion is the only thing which will 'steel the spine and nerve the arm' of the spiritually impoverished modern world for its necessary task, Cupitt affirms that all religions provide possible paths. He does, however, see Christianity as fulfilling the best in both Nietzschean humanism and in Buddhism, bringing together the radical humanist challenge of the one with the lofty spiritual attainment of the other. He assures us that after a while the grief of letting-go traditional religious understandings in favour of his radical perspective will pass. Continuity will return with the tide of Arnold's 'sea of faith', but Christianity will be transformed, serving us better once it is freed of 'illusions'.

Cupitt in 1985: *Only Human*

In this volume Cupitt consolidates his shift to a language-centred, voluntarist view of the human condition and of religion. He says it is a new kind of religious book, as it begins not from doctrine but from what has been implied about the human condition in the areas of geology and biology, psychology, social anthropology and comparative religion. It is not a philosophical anthropology; that would be the 'ghost of a theology'. No single theory could subsume the range of data anyway. With his new 'linguistic naturalism' Cupitt disposes of all forms of realism, and so all theories receive more favourable hearings as all are in some sense 'true'.

Nor does Cupitt attempt a theological anthropology; the Christian view of human nature coming to us from Genesis via Augustine is damaged beyond repair and will not survive in a post-modern world. He takes his lead from Foucault, conducting a critical reflection on the history of ideas, and from Derrida, seeking to subvert the realist illusions of Western thought. The apparent tolerance of a variety of religious positions which is becoming a feature of Cupitt's later thought points forward strongly to his next book, *Life Lines*. The view of language espoused here is taken to its conclusion in *The Long-Legged Fly*.

From covering familiar territory about science and the modern mind, Cupitt moves to consider the impact of Darwinian ideas on psychology. Darwin's removal of a privileged place for human beings in the universe is carried over into the sciences of the mind, cutting away at the pretence of rationality through the work of Freud and Jung. Cupitt spares a passing thought for the impact of such notions on our understanding of religious experience, with special reference to the extraordinarily undifferentiated states associated with mystical experiences. He decides that the experience is similar all over the world simply because it represents a suspension of the mind's normal imposition of order upon experience, involving no more than being out of one's normal wits. We find, too, a perspective on the rise of religious studies as a separate discipline, highlighting the continuing worth of religion for moderns.

We then find a strong preview of the thesis of *Life Lines*, with Cupitt arguing that particular spiritual orientations correspond to different positions in the philosophy of religion. Progress between stations in the spiritual life is made not by closer approximation to some revealed absolute, but by dissatisfaction with one's present position. We begin to see tolerance (of a sort) emerging in Cupitt, for whom language is increasingly the stuff of human world-making and not reference to any objective reality. This appears here through his set of seven ideal types (by courtesy of Eliade and Bellah) tracing human religious development to its culmination in the internalized religion of Cupitt's own voluntarism. It is explored by locating on a grid the options of dreaming (naturalistic) innocence, an Eastern 'no-self' view, a Marxist-type humanism and an ethical, eschato-logical 'Christianity'. The grid is one which Cupitt sees as fundamental, with one axis showing the extent of world affirmation or denial and the other the favouring of 'history' or alternatively 'eternity'. The question is, of course, how one chooses one of these (fairly all-encompassing) options in a world with no more absolutes. There is a risk of falling with Wittgenstein into what is for Cupitt an unacceptable quietism with no religious 'teeth'.

Finally the solution is placed in our own hands and Cupitt makes the religious point towards which he has been leading us. The old world of objective certainties having gone (at least in French philosophy departments), meaning is now to be created by us.

The creation myth in effect says, 'You can do it; here's how'; and the god functions as a guiding standard or norm. (181)

The Holy can appear so existentially real that human beings are inclined to project it out as a god but this is an illusion and the real religious imperative is to live without this 'homesickness for Being'. Faith becomes simply 'inner software' and religious ideas are for cashing only at the point of moral decision. Yet the quietism of Wittgenstein accompanying the 'death of the individual' is not to be tolerated.

Cupitt argues that we must fight back in the name of our transcendent possibilities. The limitless self of our experience, our 'I Think', is what was once called the immortal soul and is that which the mystics identify as the indwelling of God. It inspires our creativity and calls us to realize our values. It must be affirmed, as was the case when it or something like it arose as the basis of the second phase of Cupitt's early period, yet he no longer values it as highly:

A Promethean affirmation of the primacy of subjectivity is dangerous, and God and society exist to counterbalance it. . . . It (the 'I Think') must be humbled and made to pray (190).

He likens having a God before whom we can be humble without being crushed by overwhelming objectivity to the Buddhist discipline of nothingness.

Whichever representation be preferred, the function of our ideas of God, of nothingness, or of Christ's death is to stabilize the self, to hold it calm and poised in the face of the enigma of the human condition. Religion is our way of *making* sense of a life that otherwise would make no sense at all (191).

Cupitt's developing anti-Cartesian view of the world as a vast web of communication with nothing 'off the page' is in the ascendant. There is no way out of this 'flat' earth; no way forward but the critical method of hyperbolic doubt and scepticism and no way of transcendence but that of the '360° turn'. So the yearning for transcendence brings us back to the ethical, and religious belief ceases to be a separate area of human concern.

If this is a shocking idea, it is also a biblical one: when the kingdom of God arrives, the Temple and religion are at an end (196).

Articles originally from *The Listener* magazine, appended to *Only Human*, are intended to provide a summary of Cupitt's understanding of religion at this time.[13] In them, we hear the Japanese philosopher Keiji Nishitani's suggestion that Christianity now has nowhere to go but Buddhism. For Cupitt, this will ensure a new asceticism, rather than Christianity's more usual soft eudaemonism.

> We want religion to be a severe inner discipline without any consolations whatever. The colder and clearer, the better. There must be no more pixie-dust (200).

The removal of the old external validation of faith and its resultant internalization show that it was we who supported the old objective order, and not vice versa. Voluntarism is the only appropriate religious response to the resultant void.

Religion is now separate from dogma, as the Buddha, Kant and Tolstoy saw. The anti-dogmatic outlook of a post-metaphysical age can be made to serve the cause of true religion, which involves the power to 'stare down' death and nothingness.

> When we have freed ourselves of the snooping, censorious and over-scrupulous psychology of dogmatism, there is no reason at all why we should not use the resources of religion aesthetically, expressively and regulatively . . . God becomes man, the ceremonial is translated into the ethical, extraordinary charismata are given to ordinary people and diffused through common life, and God is no longer a fearsome objective Being but an indwelling spirit or guiding ideal in the heart (205f.).

For Cupitt, the Platonic vesture of Christianity must be cast off in favour of a much lighter and roomier Buddhist one.

> When the distorting influence of dogma is gone, then we post-dogmatic believers, we 'Christian atheists', see as if for the first time what religion is and what it may be in human life (206).

This has ramifications for notions of the after-life, and for Cupitt heaven and hell are now no more than states of the soul.

Furthermore, the bitter truth is that there will be no divine vengeance over the wicked and that secular myths of progress such as Marx's or that of Nietzsche's *Übermensch* offer no more comfort. Consequently, like art, religion must simply be pursued for its own sake. Christianity might then set about its task in the modern world – to unite humanism and mysticism and so to inject human value into the unprecedented spiritual poverty of the present situation.

According to Cupitt the challenge to religious voluntarism that was already present, say, in the English non-cognitivist religious philosophies of the late 1950s will not go away. Personifying God as we personify concepts like duty when saying 'duty calls' is not necessary. Nor need the Bible be seen as favouring theological realism and theistic speculation over voluntarism: as Bultmann said, 'In the Bible, God is only known as Lord'. So 'ordinary' Christianity is described by Cupitt as ' . . . a comic-book version of Platonic metaphysics for ordinary people'.

> The struggle against theological realism is then a struggle against idolatry and superstition, and for a religion that is rational and moral (212).

Therefore the two-world cosmology which has left Christians exiled from their true home for two millennia must be left behind, along with the unacceptable 'theologies' of Marxism and positivism – the one offering illusory historical progress to a better home, and the other an illusory mind-independent 'more real' external world. Mentioning the world-affirming (rather than world-denying) asceticism of the Buddha and St Cuthbert and the call for worldly Christianity by Schweitzer, Cupitt advocates the Japanese concept of the 360° turn that we came across earlier. After traversing past, present and future it returns the Christian to the present world, now able to see it and its possibilities clearly for the first time.

Cupitt in 1986: *Life Lines*

This book presents what Cupitt calls a 'Metro map of the Spirit', a diagram of which is reproduced in fig. 1. Each 'station' is at once a spirituality and a position in the philosophy of religion. None of them is privileged in relation to any absolute truth, but the intellectual and spiritual demands of post-modern life will lead the receptive believer through the stages, and particularly the 'Crisis' of stage Nine, into the realms beyond theological realism. We note too that Cupitt constantly interrupts his argument with observations on his new theme of post-modernism and his old theme of realism versus non-realism – here extended outside theology to the whole realm of human knowing. It would seem that Cupitt is feeling for a post-modern theology (hence in part the lack of 'tightness' in this and the next book, indicating the working-out of an incomplete position). All the post-realist stages presented here are dimensions of what he seeks. The search continues more fully in the next book, where many of the implications here and in the previous book are followed through.

Cupitt highlights the post-modern disappearance of that serious-ness about the meaning of life characteristic of the existentialists, and of the 'modern period' generally. He thinks it worth retrieving, believing that spiritual values remain despite the post-modern deconstruction of the self. All former certainties have broken down in a post-modern world, and beyond the collapse of the dogmatic certainties of religion we are left with only a variety of spiritual stages, linked to unfolding consciousness. Cupitt is no longer as critical of theological realists, for instance, being forced to decentre his own views in a new world where all truth is relative. He derives the stages presented here partly from traditional sources, the history of ideas, and partly from his own past. He discusses five realist and two semi-realist positions, and then a number of non-realist stages which constitute the modern religious options possible after the crisis or loss of faith – suiting a generation of 'orphans, atheists, and nomads'. The three rough tracks joining the stages are 'lines' along which the 'life energy' customarily unfolds for the Christian. There is a catholic and mystical one, an orthodox Protestant and existential one, and a liberal Protestant and ethical one. Progress is by Cupitt's way of purgation: that of religious gain through abandonment of unhelpful images.

Here Cupitt introduces his new metaphysic of the life force, which is vaguely delineated in this and his next book. In *Life Lines* it is likened to that which for the Buddha was craving, for Spinoza was *conatus*, for Hegel was *Geist*, for Schopenhauer was the will, for Nietzsche was the will-to-power, for Freud was *libido* and for

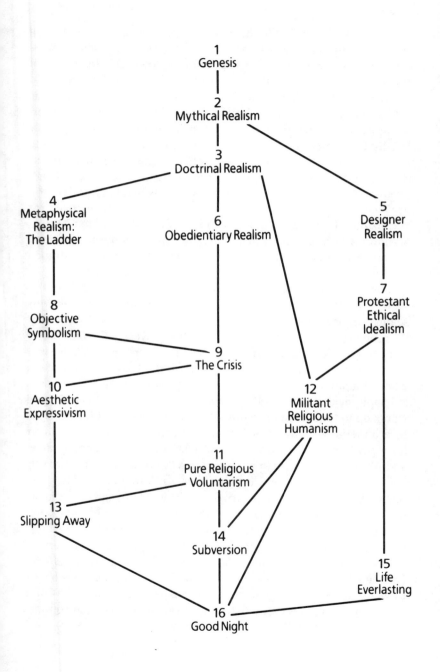

Bergson was *élan vital*. This life energy expresses itself in our growth
from an infant stage of egoism into more diversified adult personali-
ties. Myth and narrative have a special function in this formation of
the self. Cupitt defines this life energy as prior to the self/world
awareness of the individual and visible only in its representations: as
self, others and as the world itself. Despite the similarities, however,
it cannot be characterized totally according to materialist, vitalist or
idealist accounts. Since it is more fundamental than the self or the
world (and hence relativizes the whole realism/anti-realism question), Cupitt's 'life energy' brings him to a new epistemological high
ground. Being prior to the distinctions upon which logic and reason
are based, the 'life energy' is apparently exempt from any need for
verification. Cupitt goes along with it further into his later period,
attempting here and in the next book some more impressionistic and
evocative writing than that to which he has previously accustomed
us.

The first stage considered is 'Mythical Realism', the religion of
naive realists suiting the undeveloped and undifferentiated consciousness of children and members of primal societies, followed by
its more systematic 'successor', 'Doctrinal Realism'. This latter
stage is uncritical – the stuff of adolescent conversions. We have met
its weaknesses as an ideology of power in the biographical sketch,
where Cupitt referred to his own conversion to such a religion.
'Metaphysical Realism: The Ladder' follows. It is Platonic and
works up to God from the world of sense. Kierkegaard saw it as the
forerunner of Romanticism. 'Designer Realism' satisfies the hunger
for a personal God which Platonic religion could never fully meet
and is the popular layman's religion in a scientific age. It is broadly
deistic and described by Cupitt as liberal and weightless. He notes
too that some of the popularity of this position comes from its
political quietism, whereas for the new 'later Cupitt' the chief
imperative for religion today has become social change. 'Obedientary Realism' is a Protestant, moralized, adult, internalized version
of 'Doctrinal Realism', emerging at the Reformation when religion
(as seen by Cupitt) was 'blocking up the life force'. Despite its
capacity to generate powerful conversion experiences in dire
extremity, Cupitt has found that it fosters an unendurably intropunitive religious psychology.

The first form of semi-realism encountered is 'Protestant Ethical Idealism' – the sort of idealistic humanism Harnack, Schweitzer and Tolstoy would have recognized. Cupitt's misgiving is that its old-fashioned liberal hope of realizing the Kingdom of God on earth is now defunct. Nietzsche, for one, labels such idealism as spiritually poisonous, advocating instead the affirmation of life as it is and not as any idealism would prefer it to be. Cupitt also notes that the end result of this religion was to turn Schweitzer and Tolstoy into dreadful old codgers.

'Objective Symbolism' is described as catholic, and as the successor to ladder realism in an historically minded age. We recall Cupitt's mention that this was the position he held in his thirties. Such belief is aware of what religious symbols are and knows their history, yet still suspects that they symbolize *something*.

> All that remains of objectivity is the will-to-realism, a conviction that there is 'something there' which cannot be any further elaborated or justified. . . . It is repelled by the austerities of the Negative Theology, and instead casts about for some device that will enable it to cling to a realism that is in danger of being attenuated to vanishing-point (99).

Yet as we know, the 'big slovenly protean myth' of realism is dead for Cupitt. He describes this stage as the peculiar agony of the modern educated believer and moreover as a chronic faith-sickness. Instead of craving for absolute knowledge and a state in which the spirit can rest, such persons should realize that the spirit only lives and is strong when on the move.

'The Crisis' is the loss of belief in an objective God, usually accompanied by the sort of bereavement accompanying the loss of a lover (for so God and faith function in some expressions of realism). However, Cupitt mentions that persons at some stages have a relatively painless passage through the crisis, such as the 'Protestant Ethical Idealist' who easily surrenders a metaphysical God for moral values and a 'spiritual dimension in life'; or the 'Objective Symbolist' who may be just as content when 'God' becomes merely a symbol for tradition (say). (We know from elsewhere, though, just how difficult this transition has been for Cupitt himself).[14]

He sees the crisis as *par excellence* the opportunity for religious renewal. He indicates how the new life may still be seen as religious, for the re-assessment involved in the experience is ultimate or religious in character: it is a death and rebirth of the self. The new life is thus experienced as a gift, the world appears new, there is an extraordinary freedom to remake the world, religious representations are for the first time truly one's own and in addition the whole is thoroughly in keeping with the Hebraic voluntarism of the Old Testament.

'Aesthetic Expressivism' is a conservative and nostalgic view of Christianity, seen as a *techné* for living free of egoistic concern. It is romantic, making much of prayer, worship and other religious practices, all interpreted symbolically as an aesthetic and reconciling response to the world. Schleiermacher is its best advocate, in his *On Religion: Speeches to its Cultured Despisers*. Jung seems to favour it too, in his internalizing of religious meaning, and in his advocacy of the religious symbol as an agent of psychological health. R. M. Hare's non-cognitive and attitudinal Christianity is another example. A rare mention of the church by Cupitt shows that it remains alive and well even at these 'altitudes'.

> Even in the church we can now believe only in a bracketed and ironical way. But at least it can be said that our type of conscious believer lives a more unified life than could otherwise be lived, and that only within the church are to be found the resources from which one day a more integrated public culture might arise (124–5).

But he notes the danger, particularly in the post-modern age of critics and commentators, that this position makes the adherent a passive observer rather than an active creator of religious meaning – especially given its nostalgic attachment to its starting point in the tradition.

'Pure Religious Voluntarism' would appear to underlie Cupitt's own present position. It is a Christian existentialism schooled in victory over the nihil by faith and force of will, creating order *ex nihilo*. Whereas the previous position was a way of affirmation, this is one of negation. It is ultra-conscious, individualistic 'Protestantism squared', seeing 'the crisis' as the birth of real faith.

The atheistic existentialist panics and pulls out too soon, seeking to extricate himself by an act of the will before the Nihil can dissolve away the self: whereas the religious person is sufficiently disciplined to be able to wait until the end (131).

The result of this attitude is a resurgence of life energy from the depths of the nihil – the nearest Cupitt comes anywhere to a concept of 'grace'.

'Militant Religious Humanism' is about moral activism, eschewing any bourgeois individualist piety. It follows the existentialists who, finding no philosophical basis for the moral life, affirm it as a gratuitous act in defiance of tragic necessity. Cupitt mentions *The Plague* by Camus, and *The Making of the Representative for Planet 8* by Doris Lessing as novels typifying this condition.

It is central to twentieth-century experience that human beings must extract such moral and religious dignity as they are capable of directly from a clear-eyed and illusion-free recognition of the tragic nature of the human condition, and can find it in no other way (147).

We see this approach in Schweitzer's tragic programme of affirming life in the face of inevitable failure and in Bultmann's understanding of the resurrection as a dimension of the cross. The unending moral struggle involved is illuminated by Foucault's belief that given the ineradicability of oppressive power structures, every present reality must be combatted in perpetuity. Religion and its apparatus is not, however, a superfluous addition to the equipment of the secular humanist; its symbols do real work.

Religion makes a difference because it makes possible a whole-hearted commitment to action that does not become fanatical, or lead to spiritual dissipation or break down into pessimistic inactivity (151).

'Slipping Away' is the spirituality of one of those marginalized or escaping figures in a Brueghel painting who if spotted appear peripheral, but upon reflection are far more central than many others amusingly portrayed as going obliviously about their own business. Cupitt finds such figures slipping away in the last twelve novels of Iris

Murdoch. In a world where meaning and understanding have deserted us, gestures remain, including that of serving the anonymous. Iris Murdoch's saints are invisible.

At a stage called 'Life Everlasting', Cupitt examines the possibility of a world-affirming faith fully cognizant of the post-modern situation. However, he does not see any *a priori* reason why either this path or that of world-denial should be chosen in a world without foundations. He is aware of Foucault's identification of power and domination in every discourse, which can only lead to a certain scepticism and hence in a world-denying direction. Yet he feels that this conclusion is not inevitable and sets about establishing his conviction on the firmest possible foundation available in his new post-modern universe: by delineating a minimal, primal metaphysic for the life energy.

> The self-expression of that unknown reality which we have labelled the productive life-energy minimally requires that there be communication, a temporally-extended medium of communication, and subjects who are envisaged as being at least intersection-points along the lines of communication (182).

It is by assertion rather than argument that Cupitt denies that this primal metaphysic also needs extra terms about power and control *à la* Foucault, who by labelling every discourse without exception as an exertion of power would put the life energy into opposition with itself and thereby sour one's view of the world. The suggestion is that despite one's moral resolution to have no part in such abuses, they are nevertheless the compulsory adjunct of language, belonging *analytically* if you like to the very concept of communication. Cupitt, however, sides with Habermas and others who see communication as being about meaning and as being essentially eirenic. The abuses correctly identified by Foucault the Nietzschean are declared to be secondary.

Cupitt does not think it impossible that exclusivisms and similar oppressive structures might be rooted out, giving rise to more pacific and life-affirming options. This task would, of course, call for a great unlearning and indeed would be a new beginning for Western thought. Yet for Cupitt, Christianity is arguably just such a revolutionary assault on the divisions between God and man, Jew and Gentile, male and female, thus bearing the possibility of a fully reconciled humanity. Despite its many failures – condemning heretics in the name of a founder who was himself a heretic – Christianity offers a way out through its symbols. For Cupitt the decentring and dispersal of the God/man distinction is now the meaning of the incarnation – a process continuing as Christ himself is dispersed and decentred into the texts of the New Testament.

> God's death in Christ and our death in union with him, the decentring of both the Infinite and the finite subjects, may thus be seen as the means whereby the world can be saved: that is, through them we may be able to reach a spiritual state in which we can say a final and wholehearted yes to life (191).

Cupitt suggests how the resultant life might look. It is already visibly taking shape, being broadly 'green', circumventing power structures through the localizing of authority and scaling down. It is pro-environment, pro-renewable energy and favours appropriate technology. This vision of the whole rather than the parts deals better with the problem of evil and sounds loosely Buddhist. Man the communicator and his environment will interweave, producing something like the Word incarnate. (This is the programme in the next book, *The Long-Legged Fly*, in which an attempt is made to deconstruct the power claims of culture and religion, producing a properly post-modern theological text evoking these sort of values.)

At Cupitt's final station, 'Good Night', we encounter a Buddhist, post-modern version of the art of dying. The strangers peering back from old photographs of us, as well as the illusion-filled attempts of biographers to capture the essence of persons, support Cupitt's 'no-self' doctrine.

> Thus if the post-modern world is in some respects Buddhist in its metaphysics, it is also Christian. There is no substantial individual self; the human realm is a field of communicant intersubjectivity. Becoming incarnate in Christ, God enters this realm and is disseminated through it as bread and wine. He and we both lose centred subjectivity. Thus the last story we tell of our lives ought to be, not a story of the final triumph of monarchical selfhood, but a story of *kenosis*, scattering and dispersal, a self-giving and self-

loss that continue, as the hymn says, 'Till death thy endless mercies seal, and make the sacrifice complete'. If we are bold enough to call Good that Friday when darkness fell over the land because God had died in Christ on the cross, then we should be bold enough to call our own night good (198).

For Cupitt, the sole content of death is our own limitedness – an awareness forcing us back to the present.

When life is seen not as a process of self-consolidation but as a process of self-giving, emptying and sacrifice, then life can be loved in its transience, and disinterestedly. The continual loss which an open-eyed love of life involves adds a dash of anguish which heightens the flavour of our joy in life (200).

This despair of any eschatological future, fully in keeping with the proleptic understanding of Christian eschatology, is the logical consequence of Jesus' despairing cry from the cross, and for Cupitt will finally usher in the ages of faith.

Significantly, he denies that he has been 'leaning on the reader' to follow any optimum path through the stations, claiming to find all the stages perfectly licit and justifiable (though one has one's doubts!). He calls for the production of texts which help people realize their new predicament, and to be comfortable with their new life on a 'two-dimensional surface'. Just as abstract paintings are not windows to reality, but only orderings of paint on a two-dimensional surface which will, if good enough, effect a permanent change in perception, so too it is today with religious truth. There is no escaping the flat world of signs.

We read the New Testament as a story of the decentring and scattering of God, of Christ, and of the people of God: a story of diaspora. And in this long pilgrimage into diaspora, which we love and in which we find joy, lies the meaning of our life (214).

Cupitt in 1987: *The Long-Legged Fly*

Here Cupitt ventures further into the theological implications of post-modernism, attempting to produce religion and morality on a two-dimensional surface. He wishes to show that we are all word-made-flesh like Christ. This is a difficult book, highlighting the unfamiliarity of the English with the anti-philosophers and their gaze into the nihil. The interesting title is explained in an author's note as coming from Yeats' *Last Poems*

> Like a long-legged fly upon the stream
> His mind moves upon silence.

The insect in question is the pond-skater or water-strider, a creature dwelling on the two-dimensional surface of a pond or stream and making a habitable world from the interplay of vibrations variously interpreted. For Cupitt, its existence in a depthless realm of intercommunicant subjectivity is a metaphor of the spiritual and philosophical situation in a 'horizontal', post-modern world.

With Derrida, that ruthless critic of immediacy, Cupitt reminds us that there can be no abstraction away from the everyday in pursuit of 'being', and that like the painters Matisse and Monet we must discover the radiance of paradise in the ordinary.

> We have to say Yes to what is before us in all its contingency. Such is, I believe, the final message of an incarnational religion (8).

Two options are to be discussed for doing theology in such conditions. First there is 'the theology of culture', linked with the thought of Jacques Lacan. It sees the self and desire as constructed by culture within the world of signs. There is nothing outside the symbolic order. So this outlook is conservative and religiously quietistic. The alternative is 'the theology of desire', derived from the thought of the utopian Gilles Deleuze. Here the starting-point is not the strictures of culture, but rather desire trying to express itself, as in William Blake. The resultant religion is radical, humanist and utopian. It is however, emphasized that the issue between the theologians of culture and desire is not a simple question of right and wrong.

> Rather, we attempt in a text to reach a tolerably self-consistent view on a small cluster of topics: the body, desire, language, culture and faith (9).

The goal here is to produce a fully one-level theology, reflecting the combination of all things in one person symbolized by the incarnation.

> Being is reduced to meaning, meaning to evaluation, evaluation to calibrated feeling-tones, and feelings to modifications – enhancing or enervating – of the will to live (10).

Cupitt mentions his habit of beginning a book from perceived shortcomings in its predecessor. Here he notes the presence of too much dualism in *Life Lines* between the will and its representation, *à la* Schopenhauer (and Freud). A stated aim in this consciously more 'one-level' work is to remedy this, as well as to show that contrary to the quietism of a Lacanian 'theology of culture', genuine Christian innovation is still possible. A post-modern metaphysics will be consistent where its predecessors were not, and will cope best with the curse of self-reflexivity if it presents reality as a differential play of signs on a surface, like itself. It will then artistically epitomize what it propounds. A post-modern Christian metaphysics must also assert a place for creative and innovative religious action.

> Again to avoid reflexive paradoxicality and to remain at one level, the text must itself be an example of what it asserts. The text needs itself to be unshaven, embarrassing and disruptive. I am not at all confident about my capacities in this respect, but at least one can make a modest attempt to be as heretical as possible (12).

The argument begins with the denial of any super-language as sought in various ways throughout the history of Western thought. For Cupitt, ordinary language is the best we can do. As words in a dictionary refer to other words in a sideways direction *ad infinitum*, so all of our language can be understood as two-dimensional, thus cutting the nerve of realism by denying the need for any reality 'off the page'. Similarly, all former appeals for some ground of 'the moral' are denied. Since meaning is now internalized within language and its use, Cupitt favours Wittgenstein's understanding of morality as being built into our evolving language games. Far better, he suggests, to take the firmest basis for morality now available and ground it in the enhancement of the life energy. Morality should not be a harness or a bridle as in Plato but should realize the value of that which 'turns us on'. One thinks here of Spinoza and of Deleuze.

The theoretical basis of the argument unfolds further with an examination of the way in which our sense of value is tied to bodily states. Cupitt considers how evaluative scales are imprinted upon us, either by childhood discipline or through Freud's 'pleasure principle'. (Consider for example how we have learned to associate certain bodily sensations with the words 'warm and dry' and quite other sensations with the words 'cold and clammy'.) The scales combine and overlap by the use of metaphor, so that scaling and metaphorical substitution together make up our world: the one ordering and differentiating, the other unifying. Deleuze rejects all scaling with its evaluative grids as oppressive, describing the ideal individual as an autonomous metaphor-maker whose body has been totally de-territorialized of all such conditioning. However, Cupitt cannot conceive of meaning without it: 'We are going to have scales: the task is to treat them as provisional, and to criticize them' (68). This is of course very familiar, being an extension of the critical philosophy of spirit from the early period, now reappearing in the later works. Here too we encounter again the argument from *Life Lines* with Foucault as to whether language is necessarily oppressive.

A discussion of 'The Theology of Culture' sees Cupitt trying to imagine a theology faithful to Heidegger and Derrida. For him culture is what God used to be: it calls things into existence, and there is no option but allegiance. The world so envisaged is not concrete, but simply the proliferation and differentiation of entities which refer to one another for meaning, and to nothing more real outside the text. It is like the vale of *maya* in Indian thought. Culture is like God in containing nothing selfsame; it points and then moves on. The nationalist fanatics who make culture into an idol miss its religious significance, and so do those whose view of God is similar.

> So the world of meaning is nothing but a dance of difference in the Void; and *God* functions to remind us of that (107).

There is a strain of inevitability and quietism in such a view.

'The Theology of Desire' is discussed with the work of Deleuze in mind. He for one will not tolerate the former position, seen as a reactive ideology of religious conservatism. The theology of desire does not begin from a language and culture in which one is inevitably trapped, but rather with the unhindered play of desire. The body expresses it and culture orders it, differentiating and hierarchicalizing the body surface. The body is seen as created by culture out of desire. Deleuze and Guattari are utopians who resent this control by culture, labelling it fascist. (One thinks immediately of the highly determined female body and of the construction of feminine sexuality generally in our society as perhaps the best example.) For these thinkers, it is the counter-culture which expresses the cry of stifled desire, opening up new metaphors and possibilities for life.

> Thus for the theology of desire the counter-culture is the true church, and the church is the true counter-culture. It works in close alliance with art on the one hand and radical politics on the other. It contributes something that neither of them can quite provide, an experimental nursery where new body-identities and life-styles are given thorough preliminary trials before their general adoption. It has, in short, the same relationship to culture as our plant-breeding research institutes have to agri-culture (115f.).

As I mentioned at the end of Chapter I, this is the reappearance of an old idea. For Cupitt, this is fully in keeping with the basic impulse of Christianity, seen as a fundamentally anti-orthodox faith on the side of the creative potential of desire. What we found in the early Cupitt we now find again. Christianity has a unique opportunity here, over and above other religions.

'The Theology of the Cessation of Desire' brings together Cupitt's concern to affirm the flow of desire – to equate the ethical with the life-enhancing on the one hand and with support of the higher morality mentioned earlier on the other. He is no advocate of Prometheanism, hedonism or any other uncontrolled explosion of human drives. Instead, one suspects his aim is to justify a fairly traditional 'Christian' moral stance from the attenuated possibilities available to the honest thinker in a post-modern universe. Early Buddhism is just such a theology of the cessation of desire. While *Taking Leave of God* presented Buddhism as an individualistic spiritual path, Cupitt arrives significantly here with a recognition of it as a social religion. The personal dimension remains, but its goal is now more social. He likens it to the spirituality of the French structuralist Roland Barthes, which allows a certain coolness and non-egoistic detachment.

> When I understand that my self is a mere temporary aggregation of processes, and when I grasp that my own desires are part of the flux of forces in nature, then I can accept them as constituents of the whole without overestimating them (122).

Desire's own interests therefore call for a relinquishing of desire so that we are not enslaved by it. Culture gets its power from the overspill of life energy. Hence we must be careful, as Feuerbach noted, that we do not invest too much energy outside ourselves in the oppressive habit of vicarious living (there were traces of this view in Chapter 12 of *Taking Leave of God*).

> Paradoxically, you will be more fulfilled, less egoistic, less inclined to harass other people, cooler and more compassionate, if you can be content to expend your will to live just within your own life. And *that*'s the point of ascetical religion (126).

Religious practice is seen as a negotiation between the conflicting powers of desire and culture – between what for Cupitt are the daydreams of Deleuzian nomadism and the extremity of Lacan's cultural strictures. The aim here is to avoid the discontent caused by an overspill of life energy into vicarious living, which feeds culture and allows it to become oppressive. Culture then draws off more of our life energy, and so on, by a kind of ratchet effect. So Cupitt advocates what amounts to a measure of asceticism: an initial cutting-back of desire which will lead to a habitual expressing of this desire without the dissipation of vicarious living.

> My life will always be finite, but it will be a fulfilled life if I can direct my surplus life-energies into creative activity and moral struggle for human liberation.
>
> That then is the sense in which true religion teaches that after an initial death comes a progressive return of life (128).

Very cleverly, Cupitt has succeeded in combining here his affirmation of the religious primacy of the manifest and contingent, his critique of religious and philosophical realism, his liking for

Buddhism and the *via negativa* and his grounding of ethics in whatever enhances the life energy (against the 'wowserism' of much so-called 'Christian morality'), while nevertheless leaving the way open for a very conventional moral position with all its virtues of self-discipline intact – and all of this carried out while he is immersed in the epistemologically corrosive acid of post-modernism. In a classic *via media* position, redolent of Freud yet also of mainstream Anglican moral theology, Cupitt affirms both human drives *and* the constraints of culture, denying French extremists who would suppress one or the other. The root of all evil is not libido, nor is it the forces which shape us, but rather *the enslavement of desire to culture*. For Cupitt this is not inevitable, and is a condition which can be remedied particularly well with the help of Christianity.

In examining some ways in which cultural pressure prompts vicarious living, Cupitt mentions the media-dependence of our liberal society, as a result of which we must all take an interest in the affairs of strangers a whole world away. The need to create meaning, so characteristic of our times, has also led to an explosion of fiction in books and television, which provide enormous opportunities for vicarious living. Cupitt finds particularly troublesome the paradisal yearnings created by the many gratifications offered, over which much energy is wasted. (One could imagine a very conventional sexual morality built upon such apparently radical roots.)

He uses as an example the abnormal behaviour caused in herring gulls by showing them an oversized egg (to which they have no appropriate instinctual response). He mentions B. F. Skinner's observation that a cover girl is to a man what a large egg is to a broody herring gull. The result is the same; abnormal reactions are produced. Various media create such tastes for the excessive and the outrageous, and indeed culture as a whole is in the business of giving strong stimuli. Without the old idea of an examined life, it is easy for us to live vicariously through all these images. Such is the case in religion, too, and Cupitt notes the ease with which orthodox Protestantism, for instance, slips into passive media religiosity. As a result, we must become active creators of religious meaning rather than passive receivers and vicarious livers. As artists since Cezanne have been aware that they are creating rather than copying reality, so must we be aware of our creative vocation now the age of the artist-theologian has arrived.

> The church is the Christian tradition, which is a river of signs. As they flow through us, we have to take them up and make something fresh of them which will express our own desire. In this way everybody who personally appropriates Christianity and lives it does and must transmute it within his own body (146).

Cupitt then talks of Christ in the Hegelian sense of a union in one person of this world and a higher world.

> The metaphysical metaphor to which we have been led has thus become incarnational. The integral whole-body human being is one in whom flesh and spirit, feeling and meaning, are perfectly conjoined . . . It *is* the one person of the Word Incarnate, in whom two logically distinct natures or realms are conjoined 'without confusion, change, division or separation'. So we may read the Chalcedonian Definition as the manifesto of an integral religious humanism (164f.).

The sort of theological text appropriate for us will therefore be one striving to operate on one level, in which the medium and the message will coincide.

> Clearly it will not be of the older cosmic-dogmatic type. Instead it will be christological. That is, it will be made of fleshwords. By the way it is made it will seek to awaken the creative-desire-flow of the religious life that it describes (166).

Cupitt identifies Mark's Gospel as one such text, requiring us to 'fill it in'. He finishes by noting the failure of texts (including music) from the *avant garde* extremes of the 'modern period' to communicate effectively to a wide public. It seems to him that for whatever reason, melody and plot are necessary if a text is to engage our attention. But he is not in favour of the old monarchical cosmic plot upon which religion was once based, as first we saw in *Crisis of Moral Authority*. Nor does he favour the post-modern reaction to the decline of absolutes, if it leads to nothing more than ironizing, reworking and commenting on the past. For Cupitt, this alternative is too potentially dissipated to serve as a totally adequate medium for religion. He appears, in a word, uncertain.

No end-point in this search for the form of appropriate theological texts for today is therefore reached. Cupitt mentions that his intention was simply to show that all of us are flesh made word and word made flesh, like Christ.

In a recent interview, Cupitt explained his intentions in writing *The Long-Legged Fly*. Instead of demythologizing Christian doctrine into individualistic spirituality, as formerly, his aim is rather to demythologize it down into the public world of meaning where we live, the objective human world. The book was

> . . . intended as a kind of hymn to the commonness of our humanity, in which, so to say, everything happens on the skin surface. That's the point where nature and culture meet, where God becomes man, where meaning and feeling are one.[15]

III

Cupitt in Retrospect: Credibility, Adequacy, Orthodoxy

In 1984 Cupitt attacked reviewers for suggestions that he might make more of mystery and symbolism in Christianity and might thus become more 'positive' and 'constructive'. This he interpreted as a call for more obscurantism, and a greater willingness to believe ' . . . against experience, a spectacularly eudaemonistic popular metaphysics'.[1] So warned, I do not intend to open myself quite as readily to the same rebuff.

The issue is certainly cut and dried for some of his reviewers: Cupitt simply fails to measure up to some predetermined standard of orthodoxy, or perhaps even of 'revealed truth'. My sympathies are not with such an approach, and suffice it to say I take Cupitt's programme seriously enough to tackle him 'on his own turf'. Other reviewers, however, have sought to show up errors, inconsistencies and blindspots in his work, suggesting that Cupitt's conclusions are not inevitable given the assumptions he makes and the evidence he adduces. This will be my approach in this chapter. I like Cupitt and find him immensely challenging. Yet the line from *Hamlet* comes back to me: 'There are more things in Heaven and earth, Horatio, than are dreamed of in your philosophy.' This is no obscurantist flight into mystery, but rather the sober recognition that 'there is something rotten in the state of Denmark' with regard to Cupitt's religious certainties. Despite much in his rich fund of writings that is true and compelling, or at least provocative, there are also, I believe, fundamental flaws in the argument that must be brought to light. This chapter should therefore be seen as the sort of deconstructive reading Cupitt favours in his later writings. It may not be a thorough refutation, but it does at least point up the possibility that a more realist theology than Cupitt will allow might survive in the fires of the post-modern nihil.

1. Criticisms: A Credible Programme?

Straw men?

Cupitt is almost universally attacked in reviews for his descriptions of the theological realism he rejects, or indeed his descriptions of any position more conservative than his own. The religion of which he takes leave is frequently disowned by critics as a poor shadow of what they find it to be as practitioners. It is seen as a vulgar caricature of traditional theism reflecting nothing but the most dreadful extremes of popular belief and piety. So theological objectivism need not be as crass as Cupitt indicates, nor need its God be experienced as an oppressor by believers.

In the area of christology, too, sophisticated modern 'orthodox' writers might not recognize their own views among the ones attacked by Cupitt in his anti-incarnational writings of the late 1970s. It is suggested that rather than disproving christological orthodoxy, Cupitt has systematically misrepresented it, offering no better alternative.[2]

Others have noted how Cupitt tends to overstate the agreement of leading thinkers of the past with his own views. So Brian Hebblethwaite can warn that more realist interpretations of the thought of Pascal, Kierkegaard, Jung, Schweitzer and Wittgenstein are possible than *The Sea of Faith* would have us believe.[3] One reviewer quite neatly exemplifies a common reaction to Cupitt's work, combining a certain admiration that he writes so well with 'an astonishment that one who knows so much can indulge consistently in such sweeping and . . . misleading generalizations'.[4]

Cupitt's response to this is interesting;

Perhaps I do polarize the difference between traditional dogmatic Christianity and the voluntary . . . faith with which I try to replace it. But I have to do that for strategic reasons. If you describe too fully all the fine shades of opinion on the spectrum, you won't succeed in making the contrast between the two ends sharp enough.[5]

Outlandish behaviour (which I think this admission represents) has been used for emphasis at least since the days of Hosea, Ezekiel or Jeremiah. Yet the theological situation today is not so cut and dried as were the moral situations towards which prophetic books are thought to have been directed. These so-called 'fine shades of opinion' separating Cupitt's voluntarism from the naive realism of which he takes leave must presumably include all the highly sophisticated semi-realist positions characteristic of what John Macquarrie calls 'existential-ontological theism'.[6] Nowhere does Cupitt seek to engage such views, and I therefore suggest that this omission constitutes a major blind spot in his programme. Were he to contend more fully with the giants of twentieth-century theology, he would find that some of them are as dismissive of theistic and christological aberrations as he is.

We have noted Cupitt's suggestion that comparison with more 'orthodox' modern theologians such as Barth, Bultmann, Tillich, Rahner or Pannenberg would be just as disruptive of traditional theism as is his attention to such 'cognitive deviants' as the anti-philosophers. Yet is this quite fair? There is certainly a diversity in the expressions of what might be called 'orthodoxy' today, but none of them are simply arbitrary constructions. They all share an agenda set in part by the Bible and tradition, and all seek a creative reformulation of faith for the new age. I shall suggest later that in fact Cupitt shares in this task, though perhaps to a lesser extent than the systematicians he has chosen as examples. He is clearly the odd one out if joined to this list of theological names. The others are all theological realists or at least qualified realists.

In tandem with this we might wonder why the epistemologically sensitive Cupitt is not more involved in dialogue with continental hermeneutics and with its theological adaptions. Everything in Cupitt's 'spirituality' would suggest that he has nothing to fear from such goliaths as these, and I think he would do much for his credibility by confronting them. If Cupitt can cross the Channel in his most recent writings to court the radical Parisians, he would do well to widen his itinerary and include the best of recent continental systematics and hermeneutics as well.

One suspects, however, that Cupitt will not follow this advice, as these areas are not 'where the action is' for him at present. His aim appears to be not the securing of any particular position, but rather simply the pursuit of his vision of the spiritual and the moral world.[7] Such an assessment of his aims is supported by Cupitt's frequent declarations that he will be judged by history.

The danger in such an approach is that of placing oneself outside beyond the reach of falsifiability – a danger that should put any scientifically-minded scholar on his guard. One can never be too critical, and if Cupitt is convinced that he has the critical game sewn up, he must then begin to ask meta-critical questions in order to deconstruct his own biases, not least of which is his quasi-positivistic limiting of the range of admissible evidence for theological reflection. This is particularly true when one considers the spectre of inerrancy present in Cupitt's critical philosophy of spirit. If Cupitt in his theology is at 'the end of the world'; if his position is the one which (allowing the greatest freedom to break idols) cannot be surpassed, then he is in a sense *free of his own criticisms*. In removing religious illusions, his axis is away from church, dogma and 'Platonic religion' so that no foreseeable criticism from these directions would need to be taken seriously. Somewhere, Cupitt describes 'Platonic religion' as a protective device against falsification, yet his own programme and conclusions can have a similar effect. There is therefore a sense in which Cupitt places himself beyond criticism, by standing unassailably alongside 'the Last Man'. This, I suggest, is reflected in his general unwillingness to give his critics a thorough reply.[8] Some implications will be considered in what follows.

Autonomy and heteronomy: a false distinction?

The unquestioned favouring of autonomy over heteronomy in human life and in the evaluation of theism is not as obvious as Cupitt would have us believe, following Kant, in whose view ' . . . acceptance of a positive revelation of supra-rational truth would subject us to an odious *despotism of mystery*'.[9] Such an attitude seems to equate obedience with sin – a reversal of more usual considerations. Yet few would question the value of obedience to parents, teachers, wise customs or to the due process of law. Such attitudes can in fact foster an integrated personality if rightly approached as part of an authentic, 'owned' commitment.

It simply cannot be maintained that all external limitations are stifling and immoral. One can consent to them freely, thus preserving autonomy and even enhancing one's scope for creativity. The artist, for instance, in choosing certain materials must of necessity exclude others, so that all creativity takes place within some self-imposed limits. After all, the considerable restrictions of sonnet form were hardly a grave imposition on Shakespeare, while the range of new dynamics available to composers after Cristofori invented the pianoforté have hardly made the rich corpus of harpsichord music redundant!

In addition, Cupitt's position exalts individualism more highly than our sense of needing one another will allow, as we shall see later when considering the practical adequacy of Cupitt's religion. Exalting autonomy as an unquestioned absolute ignores how human fulfilment usually comes through right dependence.[10] This is true in all relationships within the family, society and the economy. Indeed, in his novel *Crime and Punishment*, Dostoevsky uses his deluded and ultimately ineffectual character Raskolnikov to illustrate the limitations of autonomous modern personhood. The insights of Kierkegaard into individualism and the danger of absorption in the mass of humanity need therefore to be tempered by the insights of modern sociology and the central I-Thou polarity of Buber's personalism, though we may note that the later more socially-aware Cupitt is redressing this over-dependence on the notion of autonomous individualism.

As John Hick and John A. T. Robinson point out, too, with respect to theism, atheism on the one hand or obedience to a cosmic tyrant on the other do not exhaust the options available to modern religious thought.[11] Because he finds no 'disclosivity of the sacred' within the human condition or in the world, no natural theology, Cupitt seems to think that realist theism depends on an arbitrary revelation, which would be as odious as it is questionable. But what of the 'semi-realist' middle ground mentioned previously as 'existential/ontological theism' and its modest natural theology? Meaningful and religiously productive God-talk is possible between the extremes of naive realism and Cupitt's constructivist voluntarism, though as we have seen Cupitt's dismissal of what he calls 'liberalism' sweeps away these possibilities.

Realism versus constructivism?

In favouring constructivism over realism in his view of 'world-making', Cupitt of course opens himself to all the classical philosophical arguments surrounding this dispute. The later Cupitt sees morality and eventually the world at large as human constructions. Yet with regard to religion and the task of the 'artist theologian' to create it for himself, Cupitt's constructivism is ambivalent – not quite the *creatio ex nihilo* we would associate with his views in the other two areas mentioned here.

First, in his haste to deny that *morality* is externally grounded and can be read off either from nature or from scripture, Cupitt over-compensates with constructivist suggestions that we make our own morality. Yet surely our morality arises *in response to* givens in our world, the tradition in which we live, our personal past and so on;[12] givens which come not least from significant others during our upbringing.

> Moral development is not plausibly represented as an advance towards the condition in which a will with no (acknowledged) history invents its values and determines its policies in a social vacuum.[13]

Secondly, as regards the view that *religion* is a construction – the stuff of projection alone, having nothing to do with external reality – we can at least 'hedge our bets'. (After all, Cupitt does so himself in *Taking Leave of God* with his Tillichian-sounding hint of a 'God behind God'.) A usual rejoinder to all projection theories is that the source of beliefs and the validity of beliefs are separate things. That religion involves projection need not disprove the existence of the object of religion – fully human and historically evolved symbols may still have an extra-human reference. The sociologist Peter Berger is one writer sensitive to this issue. He identifies mathematics as an example of a man-made edifice which nevertheless exhibits great predictive power in the non-human world.[14] Despite a long debate in the philosophy of the discipline, mathematics seems in a sense to be *discovered* as well as *invented*.

Yet we must be careful not to misunderstand Cupitt when he speaks of religious belief as constructed by each believer. This is not to say that he favours the rejection of Christian tradition entirely, advocating instead the creation of religious meaning totally 'from scratch'. Far from it. We shall see later that Cupitt's programme is not dissimilar to that of the constructive theologian – one who reinterprets Christianity for a new age. Recently, in fact, Cupitt has described the Christian tradition as a river of signs which flow through us, and of which we must make something fresh. But he likens this task to what painters have known at least since Cezanne, that the creative reinterpretation is what matters, and not the object painted.[15]

So just how constructivist is Cupitt with respect to religion? His openness to the tradition suggests some ambivalence here, and even his likening of Cezanne to the modern theologians is worded ambivalently: although construction of religion by 'the subject' is presented as what matters, the status of 'the object' is unclear. That all perception is theory-laden is, of course, a basic premise for Cupitt: no reality is ever 'taken neat'. Brian Russell points out, however, that someone who has never drunk gin neat may nevertheless have at least a hint of its flavour from drinking gin and tonic.[16] Similarly, that Cezanne 'constructed reality' is not an unreasonable conclusion, yet he did not do so in a vacuum. There is still an external world with which he interacts, one piece of which is recognizable in his no fewer than sixty paintings of Mont Ste Victoire! So, too, the artist theologian constructs religious reality, but not in a void.

Thirdly we come to the denial of any realism whatever in the *'complete constructivism'* of Cupitt's most recent writings: it is not only fiercely problematic in its own right but is also hard to reconcile with the 'incomplete constructivism' of his views about religion that we have just considered. For one thing it is not obvious to Fergus Kerr[17] that Wittgenstein is quite the 'linguistic naturalist' Cupitt claims him to be. Kerr suggests that for Wittgenstein words grow from and express forms of life in a way Cupitt will not admit, and that the general facts of physical and psychological nature set constraints upon our power to generate meaning. For Cupitt to begin building his recent views of the world as totally constructed within language from Wittgenstein is therefore problematic. In addition, we note that a theory of 'complete constructivism' denying realism of any kind is not falsifiable[18] and therefore not exactly in keeping with a rigorous scientific spirit. Maurice Wiles notes that on this issue Cupitt is as impossible to argue with as an extreme Freudian or Barthian. He suggests that thoroughgoing constructivism is more implausible than some form of critical realism.[19] A genuine act of faith is called for to believe that nothing exists outside the mind.

A lingering metaphysics?

Earlier I argued that the continuing presence of the transcendent in Cupitt's programme had realist implications beyond his taking leave of God. In his earlier period Cupitt distinguished the God-of-the-programme from the 'real God'. Yet this distinction left ontological links between the 'two gods' uncertain. For instance, it is unclear in *The Leap of Reason* whether the transcendent is an intellectual/imaginative standpoint to be adopted by the believer, an external reality or perhaps a bit of both.[20] And with respect to *Taking Leave of God* I have raised questions about the status of Cupitt's 'God beyond God'. Yet epistemological questions are inevitable when we ask how human religious creations can point to an unknown God. Against what standard do we choose which images to affirm or negate, or choose between different religions? As Maurice Wiles goes on to ask: 'If religious images are so incommensurate with the transcendent reality to which they point, how are we to criticize them?'[21] Furthermore Cupitt says it is religiously appropriate to think there might be a totally unknowable transcendent mystery beyond the God of theism.[22] Elsewhere in the same book, however, he describes any speculation about a non-religious reality of God as religiously vulgar and immature. How is such a speculation even allowable?

Nor is the later Cupitt free of a fuller metaphysics than he will admit. Despite claims that it is only an heuristic device,[23] the life energy placed so centrally in his recent books sounds for all the world like a metaphysical, foundational *something*. And as regards

Cupitt's 'religious requirement', Keith Ward observes: 'The ontology of the mechanistic world allows no place for these free-floating mysterious "demands", made by nobody upon everybody.'[24] The question, then, has been well and truly posed: what sort of crypto-realist is Cupitt?

What sort of 'requirement'?

What, then, is the basis of Cupitt's religious requirement?[25] We may also wonder whether submission to the religious requirement involves any less heteronomy than submission to an external force, just because the 'God pole' is internalized. Cupitt rejects as spiritually harmful a God who actually 'exists', and yet it appears that all the excesses of a realist theism disappear the moment this God is internalized, becoming ' . . . a unifying symbol that eloquently personifies and represents to us everything spirituality requires of us'.[26] *Prima facie*, this is a contradiction. How is it that the 'laundering of God' involved in this process of internalization turns a 'spiritual ogre' into an acceptable religious image? Keith Ward is not entirely off the mark when he calls Cupitt an apostle of heteronomy after all, ' . . . grovelling odiously before stern and unbending duty'.[27] What is internalized is not necessarily less oppressive than what is external. Herein lies the particular insidiousness of brainwashing, for instance, where the oppressor becomes an internal voice, so gaining even greater hold over the victim. Many people in our secular, post-Christian society have thoroughly internalized the God-images of their childhood and yet are no better off for it. Nor is it obvious that the internalized 'Gods' of the various post-realist stages in *Life Lines* are necessarily more liberating and spiritually enobling than those of more realist stages. (And it is even questionable whether persons at the stage of 'mythical realism' – corresponding in *Life Lines* to the infant or 'primal' state – could have a sufficiently unified personality even to register anything as all-encompassing as Cupitt's religious requirement.)

Why, after all, is this religious requirement any more dependable than conscience, which need reflect no more than ingrained 'herd instinct'?[28] I have a vegetarian friend whose conscience troubles him about wearing leather shoes – a practice which, I would suggest, would not offend most morally serious people. So conscience is no infallible guide; nor is the religious requirement. Many are led by their version of it into bizarre religious practices, beyond any accountability. Furthermore, what of Cupitt's critical-ethical principle of the rigorous, deconstructive questioning of presuppositions? How can the religious requirement be so pure a part of us, free of any cultural or other taint?

For Rowan Williams, the most disappointing thing about Cupitt's work is its predominant rhetoric of power: ' . . . if we are to avoid seeing ourselves as puppets of the divine will, it seems, God must become the tool of the finite will'.[29] Yet it is not obvious that God is necessarily a rival claimant for power, leading to a Feuerbachian diminution of the self. Why is a religious requirement more in keeping with healthy human autonomy than willingly and consciously submitting oneself in freedom to some external God? Such a God might well be far less 'heteronomous' than the overwhelming demands of the various types of religious requirement which people might experience.

Why religion?

Cupitt believes in religion, though he does not believe in God. He affirms the necessity of religious practices throughout his books; even the hard and resilient hyperboreans of *The World to Come* need the life-support systems of religion to sustain them in their chilly climes. Yet establishing this need is problematic. D. H. Lawrence and T. S. Eliot had similar backgrounds, but one saw religion as necessary for the spiritual life and the other did not.[30] Similarly, what is perhaps the best philosophical treatment of the human condition to date, that of Sartre, has no need for God.[31] My question then is: if we modern readers of Cupitt are 'tough enough' to be Hyperboreans, with some more toughening would we graduate to being Sartreans, rejecting religion altogether? If, as Cupitt suggests in *Taking Leave of God*,[32] God as a principle will come to replace God as a person in the process of our becoming spiritually more mature, why should further spiritual growth not allow us to dispense with God-talk altogether? In defence Cupitt might recall the spiritual dance of denial and affirmation which we first met in our discussion of *The Leap of Reason*, but this is denial and affirmation *of a particular system within religion*, and *not of religion itself*. This particular dancer therefore remains religious wherever he steps. Yet what is to stop him dancing away into irreligion, save for the arbitrary intuitionism of Cupitt's protestations?[33]

Christian Buddhism?

Keith Ward among other critics would remind Cupitt that Buddhism is more than a spirituality. It is a doctrinal religion, and Cupitt is mistaken if he thinks it will support his non-dogmatic Christianity.[34] Yet this is to misunderstand the selectivity of the early Cupitt in his use of Buddhism. We have in fact heard him assert that it is the form rather than the content of Buddhism upon which he depends. The later Cupitt, however, is more attracted to Buddhist ontology, adopting the doctrines of no-self, a real void, etc. Moreover the interest in a cool and detached spirituality remains, despite Cupitt's attempts in *The Long-Legged Fly* to make it more social.

Notwithstanding the large areas of possible rapprochement between Buddhism and Christianity as illustrated, for instance, by Hans Küng in his book *World Religions: A Dialogue*, it is not obvious that they are quite as compatible as Cupitt suggests. A religion of *nirvana* (extinction) and of *sunyata* (emptiness) is not altogether compatible with a 'hotter', more involved religion of *sōtēria* (salvation) and *plērōma* (fullness). As Dubarle puts it, Buddhism so conceived

> is undoubtedly the picture of a very high level of spirituality, capable of producing – as in fact happens – a very pure morality, an extreme courage of will and, at the same time ... an equilibrium in the practice of life which is as sensible as it is simple, on principle detached from every excess, even in a life ardently and persistently vowed to the quest for spiritual liberation. But at the same time, at least for the Christian, the picture is one of a spirituality lacking divine intimacy and the joy of creation, despite so many aspects ... that seem to resemble Franciscan spirituality. It also lacks St Francis' song of the creatures. It is a spirituality of fascinating but harsh distances, a spirituality of the self-dependent ... that knows no more – or can find no more – than itself, and which is determined not to depend on anything but itself. It is a spirituality of stoic or Pelagian parentage we would say in the West.[35]

Finally, here we note that Cupitt favours the 'less religious', 'more philosophical' earlier and hence 'purer' Theravada form of Buddhism: the religion of the self-possessed *Arhat* rather than the outgoing *Bodhisattva*. It is an altogether more Protestant form of Buddhism. But the softening of this form in the rise of Mahayana indicates the need within Buddhism for a 'warmer', less stark expression. If most Buddhists now pursue some form of the Greater Vehicle, having left Therevada behind, why should the Lesser Vehicle appeal any more to Christians?

A tolerant Cupitt?

In Cupitt's later period a certain tolerance of conflicting religious positions develops though no one who has read *Life Lines* will have missed the obvious criticism of the realist stages, suggested at least by placing them low in an order of development. Cupitt, too, has exalted heresy and dissension as valuable in their own right, yet he would certainly come down hard on religious ideas he found silly or unhelpful, without of course using the language of heresy or of dogmatic orthodoxy. The Cupitt who gave charismatics a thorough drubbing in a 1976 article 'The Charismatic Illusion' would not, I suspect, be loading the Emmanuel College chapel card with fundamentalist or charismatic preachers, despite any new-found tolerance. The old Anglican equation of bad taste with sin has surely not been overturned.

The problem lies in the way in which Cupitt shifts the criteria of religious truth from the dogmatic to the aesthetic.[36] If this is meant to suit a newly beliefless religion better, then it forgets how ideologically loaded aesthetics can be, as for instance in the area of art appreciation. It forgets, too, that the aesthetic categories of beautiful and ugly have never been very far from the 'dogmatic categories' of true and false. So a mathematical proof or solution will often be spoken of as 'elegant' or 'beautiful', while an aesthetically superb and *disclosive* art work might well be described as 'true to life'. If Cupitt thinks to end the conflicts of dogmatism by recourse to aesthetic categories, then he must never have read conflicting film reviews.

In *The Sea of Faith* Cupitt began to describe religious beliefs as concerned with what constitutes the best view of the human condition, having long abandoned any hope they might refer to what might objectively be the case 'supernaturally'. Yet here, too, a plurality of views compete to explain the human condition – with competing psychologies, political ideologies, and so on – so that diverting the search for religious meaning into this particular arena does not guarantee any escape from dogmatism either.

Dogmatic scepticism?

First, over Jesus in the Bible, Cupitt is often accused of being too selective in his reading of the New Testament evidence. There are many arguments against Cupitt's attitude to the historical Jesus as expressed in his anti-incarnational writings of the late 1970s, not least of which is Turner's observation that Jesus is never encountered 'pure' in the New Testament but always through a tradition of interpretation.[37] Given the later Cupitt's departure from his exclusive dependence on the historical Jesus, however, I suspect that he has learned some of these lessons and moved on. But it is not obvious that incarnational mythology is as baseless and unworkable as Cupitt would have us believe.

Sebastian Moore highlights a mistake made by the whole 'myth of God incarnate' school in their claim that high christology was a late development.[38] A high christology is in fact in place as early as Paul (and according to source criticism, well before). But it was a *functional* christology, which then grew more slowly into the developed 'Christendom synthesis' so vilified by Cupitt (though there are many New Testament roots of later christological orthodoxy as identified, for instance, by Graham Stanton).[39] It would appear certain that even before the Gospels were written, Christian faith had become focussed on the person of Jesus. It is not obvious that this is a bad thing, nor is it obvious from Cupitt's own high view of Jesus that he is altogether rid of the 'taint' of kerygmatizing himself. The fulsome quotations included at the end of Chapter I give the game away, with Cupitt displaying the same tendencies of elaboration that I suspect were motivating the early Christians as they illustrated their new theistic faith with reference to the man who had made it so real for them: ' . . . the man whose significance for Christianity was transmitted in the form of the incarnational myth'.[40] This suspicion is heightened when we see the extent to which even the later Cupitt has recourse to the historical

Jesus, despite the almost total impossibility of verification. How, for instance, can Cupitt know that Jesus was the first to see the tremendous religious possibilities of the nihil?[41]

The shift of the later Cupitt from a liberal historical Jesus to a sort of 'Christ' – that is to say, to a spiritual principle – is obvious. Fully orthodox christology, therefore, is not the only sort for which the historical basis is less secure than its proponents might wish! So despite its more recent retreat from historical considerations, Cupitt's own christology *still* demands much from the historical Jesus. But this cannot be delivered with any historical certainty.

We might ask, too, why it is that Cupitt's favoured myths about Jesus – the apocalyptic myth in which he allegedly lived and even the Johannine pre-existence myth which Cupitt is prepared to class as an ally[42] – are any more acceptable for him than is the incarnational myth.

> Christologies which are not against us are with us. Will (Cupitt) not consider turning incarnation Christologies – at least the more thoughtful ones – into allies rather than enemies? Is he so sure that the task here would be so much more difficult than it is in those cases where he anticipates success, e.g. in the case of apocalyptic or wisdom mythology?[43]

One cannot help but conclude that Jesus and the Christ remain something of a surd in Cupitt's arithmetic.

The second issue to be raised under this heading of 'dogmatic scepticism' is Cupitt's attitude to developed doctrine. It is obviously not the case that doctrine is an unqualified evil for Cupitt. We hear again and again how valuable various doctrines are as picturesque reinforcements, etc., in the spiritual life, and we encounter quite a lot of doctrine in various states of demythologization throughout Cupitt's work. What is unacceptable is any realist view of doctrine. Where there is no danger of this, even the traditional attributes of God can be appraised for their religious value, as in *Taking Leave of God*. I think the problem lies in a confusion of doctrine with dogma. Doctrine would appear to be allowable in Cupitt's schema, becoming dangerous only when granted unquestioned, dogmatic status. But what advocate of a liberal 'theology from below' would have any serious difficulty with this? Seeing doctrines as symbolic and man-made, one can imagine a liberal Christian who would certainly reject any uncritical notion of the unquestionable, supernatural origin of doctrine. Yet he would still have sufficient confidence in the power of these doctrines to illuminate the human condition in the light of the experience of transcendence to be as it were *dogmatic* about them, though of course in this weaker, more sceptical sense.

Nor is it obvious that Cupitt is any different. We have seen how 'dogmatic' he can be about his own understanding of doctrine and indeed of favourite individual doctrines as well. What has become of the notion of the regulative truth of doctrine characteristic of his early fondness for Mansel? No doubt it is still here, though obscured by the confusion between doctrine and dogma I have sought to demonstrate.

Nor can it be said with Cupitt that the formulation of doctrine is the fruit of idle speculation alone, as suggested in parts of *Taking Leave of God* and elsewhere. If one wishes to be *scientific* in fact, might not some speculation about the ultimate ground of it all be at least an allowable feature of 'good religion'?

> The success of the sciences is the best argument for theism there is, for it leads us to seek ever more complete explanations of things.[44]

The instinct which drives doctrinal development is not, I suggest, adequately refuted by Cupitt. We have seen how christological speculation was a part of the response of New Testament Christianity to the impact of divine reality focussed in Jesus. It was certainly speculative in part, but still religiously serious enough to outweigh Cupitt's objections. To deny this is to deny Max Weber's understanding of the history of a religious tradition as involving the 'routinization of charisma' – an apparently inevitable process of 'settling down', involving the development of doctrine. Cupitt fails to reckon with the impact on the New Testament churches of the delay of the parousia, the rise to dominance of Gentile Christianity and all other forces then and since which have forced Christianity to inculturate itself and, as C. S. Lewis puts it somewhere, 'to settle down for the long haul of history'. I would argue, therefore, with regard to christology for instance, that the Christ is no less a critical stimulus, no less religiously evocative and indeed no less the fulfilment of all Cupitt's hopes for the historical Jesus just because he now lives in the kerygma. Besides, it is not obvious that purity is a function of antiquity in matters ecclesiastical or christological. Indeed doctrine can highlight those dimensions of religion which Cupitt finds laudable rather than invariably obscuring them, as he seems to suggest. In the case of Bultmann, for instance, the kerygma is no attempt to fend God off, but rather allows the existential reality of the cross to find some purchase in modern lives. Surely this is also Cupitt's intention?

A further issue is raised by Helen Oppenheimer, who is perhaps echoing Sebastian Moore. She considers it incredible that in his contribution to *The Myth of God Incarnate* Cupitt is not more sensitive to the Byzantine pictures of Christ he so despises.[45] The great power they exude does not necessarily represent that of the Roman state but with a little imagination can be understood as saving power over all the spiritual ills with which Cupitt would contend. Fr Moore in fact seeks to understand this power in depth-psychological terms.[46]

> Surely it may be said, on behalf of Christians who are not experts, that the great figures of Christ Pantocrator have a more authentic religious impact than this. I have recently had the chance to revisit the one at Daphni. If there is a high Christology here, and however it got here, its portrayal is profoundly and solidly human with no imperial trappings. Or one could instance the superlative picture of the risen Christ in the Kariye Djami in Istanbul, heaving Adam and Eve from their tombs like lie-a-beds. The majesty of this figure is not obviously related to the Byzantine court.[47]

What is wrong with these pictures being allowed to join Cupitt's allowed doctrines as 'picturesque reinforcements' of the spiritual life?

Finally, let it be said that dogma and doctrine do not necessarily entail naive realism. A whole range of semi-realist theologies far more tolerant of 'the tradition' nevertheless share with Cupitt his concern to bring religion up to date.

In conclusion, however, it should be noted that here and elsewhere the as-yet incomplete programme of Cupitt's later period already sets aside various features of the early period which have attracted criticism. In *The World to Come*, for instance, we have met a willingness to find in the symbol of the exalted Christ an image of the world to come. This greater openness suggests that some of these criticisms might one day be out of date.

2. Criticisms: An Adequate Religion?

Realistic about the human condition?

In his book *The Emergent Church*, J. B. Metz tells how he asks his (German) students whether their theology is robust enough to survive the challenge of Auschwitz. Such a concern highlights the importance for theology of the problem of evil and its calling into question the myth of human perfectibility. The early Cupitt would have had little need for such a warning but the later Cupitt in *The World to Come* must beware the danger of talk about human possibilities, especially if the best illustration available is the (alleged) altruism of the blood donor. Note in tandem with this Cupitt's failure to make any sense out of a surprisingly powerful and attractive theological idea from the past, what Aulén called 'the classical theory of the atonement' in his book *Christus Victor*. It is not merely a crass military model,[48] just as the Byzantine Christ figures have a power which is not merely political and spiritually oppressive.

Adequate to Christian experience?

Contrary to Cupitt's voluntarism, the will is not the centre of the psyche nor is it necessarily the most important religious 'faculty'. As Simone Weil put it, reflecting on an over-abundant exercise of 'the will' in the history of our times: 'We have to cure our faults by attention and not by will.'[49] For Rowan Williams, however, Cupitt is apparently unaware of this, placing the contemplative and the ethical in sharp distinction.[50]

Quasi-mystical talk of love as a way of knowing typical of Roman Catholic theology would probably sound like empty fideism to Cupitt, yet reducing Christianity to a project to be carried through by the self denies the whole experience of encounter with and dependence on the transcendent, so central to Christian under-standing. Instead of a demanding religious requirement, many Christians share with C. S. Lewis the experience of being 'surprised by joy'. Now Cupitt's religious requirement may be considered gracious in so far as it enables moral progress, but such sparse language seems rarely to have been thought adequate to the task of explaining life in what Ricoeur called 'the economy of unearned fulfilment'. Unless like Cupitt one is somewhat of a Pelagian ('The most abiding creed of the English') it is not likely that the realities to which Christian God-talk witnesses will present themselves as a task rather than a gift. The order is important. Nor is the modern world quite so bleak as Cupitt suggests for many, if not most, Christians. Another Christian insight, encoded in the doctrine of Creation, is that human beings *can* feel at home in the cosmos. Perhaps without this feeling theological realism would not have survived.

Too much self?

Keith Ward and other critics were right to point out the anomaly in Cupitt's early period of an allegedly tough and anti-eudaemonistic religion which is, in reality, a self-help project. *Taking Leave of God*, for instance, is very individualistic, as we have seen, and locates the 'saving of one's soul' at the centre of Christian priorities. But whereas Cupitt can admit that the moral quest collapses as soon as it becomes self-regarding,[51] it is not until his later period that he frees himself from a parallel mistake in the realm of religion. There is obviously more to religion than the needs of the self, the 'salvation' of which is seen by Christianity at its best to be but the by-product of a life of worship and service. As Rowan Williams put it:

> 'I want nothing but Jesus and to see him at peace in Jerusalem' (the prayer of Hilton's 'pilgrim') means something other than 'I want to be a fulfilled autonomous spiritual subject'.[52]

That the later Cupitt has answered these criticisms however was evident in a recent interview:

> Christianity has got to leave its individualistic tradition behind. The object is not to save yourself but to give your life.[53]

In the more recent 'public' Cupitt there has been a decentring of the religious subject to go with his earlier decentring of the idea of God. What John Bowker called 'the man of the gaps'[54] and what Rowan Williams identified as a 'pre-linguistic core of pure selfhood'[55] were a feature of the first flush of Cupitt's post-realist thought, whereas his new metaphysics of the sign and the life energy suggest otherwise.

For 'real people'?

Is Cupitt's religion too high-and-dry, too intellectual or in other ways too demanding for 'ordinary people'? Can we imagine on Cupitt's lips the words 'Come unto me all ye who labour and are heavy laden, and I will give you rest'? As Williams rightly observes, if the work of religion is to celebrate the victory of universal free and sovereign consciousness, then faith is presented as the enemy not only of belonging but of need – even finitude.[56] It is also claimed that Cupitt fails to appreciate the grind of everyday living and the consequent need for spiritual comfort, the lack of which would make his religion irrelevant and inaccessible to ordinary folk.[57]

No matter whether one is Hyperborean or not, the call in Cupitt's works for purity and disinterestedness is problematic. The demands of morality are such that the most promising avenues of one's own moral perfection sometimes need to be surrendered,[58] as Dietrich Bonhoeffer no doubt discovered.[59] One may recall, too, the constant reminders of the advocates of social justice that our ease in the West (by which we have the luxury of thoroughly pursuing these dilemmas) is bought at the price of much suffering in the Third World. How then can we be satisfied with any purity and disinterestedness we might cultivate?

For whom then?

In one sense the answer is obvious: those whose needs have been met by the earlier stations along their 'life lines' and who are ready to pass through the fires of the nihil are the ones for whom Cupitt's programme is appropriate. For this reason, if for no other, Cupitt's will never be a popular religion. In a sense it dogmatizes the modern person,[60] appealing to that relatively small group (historically and geographically) of disaffected Christian intellectuals who could hardly be called representative (though one suspects that Cupitt's following among the lapsed churchgoers whom clergy seldom see might be surprising). Yet there are those, mentioned in *Life Lines* and elsewhere as easily negotiating 'The Crisis', who seem to have no difficulty with Cupitt and who need not be disaffected intellectuals. Peter Mullen is obviously one such:

> Now the whole trouble is, of course, that the couching of religious experience in psychological terms is regarded as reductionism, as the abolition of religion – as atonality and then serialism were for a time regarded as the end of music. And, as in the case of music, the attendant fears are groundless.[61]

Rabbi Dan Cohn-Sherbok is another. He identifies Cupitt's programme with that of Mordecai Kaplan and the Reconstructionist school within Judaism, though we note that Jewish identity is far more racial and far less 'doctrinal' than is Christian identity.[62]

Another criticism I have heard levelled not only at Cupitt but at all theology with an agenda set by modern English philosophy is that it reeks of comfort and privilege, disporting itself as it were between the senior common room and the well appointed study without ever once encountering the 'real world'. (Recall for instance the distinction made by Kosuke Koyama between theology done at 70° and theology done at 120°.) The suggestion here is that it is easier to cope with a depersonalized and evacuated religion such as that of Cupitt when one lives 'comfortably'. Such a theology would never, we are told, present itself to a third-world Christian (say), who instead of doing theology in a room overlooking an Oxbridge quad would have to work out his or her theology in the context of a struggle for liberating praxis.

Two things militate against this over-simple and rather smug conclusion. The first is that congenial surroundings, while perhaps allowing more opportunity for reflection, are no guarantee of spiritual comfort. This is in fact so obvious it should not need to be stated. The second is that the 'tough and ascetical' proponents of such criticisms themselves do, at the end of the day, live in very comfortable *cognitive* worlds, untroubled by the real challenges of the philosophy of religion. How easy to practise physical ascesis when one's intellectual needs are all met! Try to reverse the order, however, and we have seen what happens. So the sort of theology under attack is not totally explicable as a parlour-game for the comfortable. That criticism could, I think, fall at least as readily on conservatives as on radicals. Indeed, much conservative religion is a flight from the confusions and pluralities of modern life; an ecclesio-spiritual resort of unmatched comfort compared with the sparsely furnished cognitive universe of the radical theologian in which he dwells at chilly, hyperborean temperatures.

It has been suggested, too, that Cupitt's religion suits capitalists. Rowan Williams hints at this and Denys Turner goes on to mention the Marxist critique that autonomy is really a cover-up for heteronomy and that Cupitt's language displays just the sort of influences that advanced secularizing capitalism would impose upon religious discourse.[63] It is Fergus Kerr, however, who most forcefully drives the point home.

> This Kantian picture of the self-legislating individual retains its hold on the modern Liberal imagination, albeit in forms that would have horrified Kant himself. The person who prides himself on being the Captain of his own soul is the buccaneer of the free-enterprise market economy, the freebooting entre- preneur in his privateer who imposes his own rules on the immense void of faceless sea.[64]

Again we must note that the later Cupitt is far less susceptible to this form of criticism.

Finally, in considering whom Cupitt's religion 'suits' (if anyone), let us look to Cupitt himself. I have noted six occasions in his work where he refers to the personality of an individual to explain his theology, not to mention the indelible link established between personality and theology at least since *Life Lines*. The same ap- proach can, of course, therefore be made to Cupitt. He shares with the many tragic heroes of *The Sea of Faith* Petru Dumitriu's inability to see the world as a home, at least until the considerable freeing-up of the later period. Charles Pickstone succeeds in illuminating the situation of the early period with a highly illustra- tive and successful comparison of Cupitt with the painter Piet Mondrian. He suggests that Cupitt's writing manifests the same puritanical, will-dominated, unsacramental spirit of Mondrian's paintings. Of these he says that:

> they are a sort of parody of Calvinistic spirituality: disciplined, logical, austere and unsentimental, truthful to the materials used

and without illusions; but in their purity they are entirely unsacramental. Admittedly, they speak of the universal, but only of its abstract expression, unfleshly and unincarnational.[65]

Pickstone's assessment of Mondrian also serves to highlight some of the difficulties with Don Cupitt's religion, or at least with that of his early period:

> Mondrian's abstraction, will dominated and discarnate, lacks the element of love, of the acceptance of constraints, the curves of give and take, that a more complete view of man compels us to supply.[66]

3. Cupitt's Orthodoxy: Atheist Priest?

The English background

For David L. Edwards, the presence of so anomalous a being as Don Cupitt in the English church highlights all of its difficulties with theology. He mentions how the General Synod is peopled with neo-conservatives, for whom a theological issue is whether a woman can be a priest, or whether union with Protestant churches can proceed without their moderators accepting ordination to the episcopate. There appears to be little energy or interest for the tackling of hard theological issues. So what is to be made of a priest who, by any dictionary definition at least, is an atheist?[67] Part of the problem is to be located in the ambivalence of the Anglican tradition towards theological inquiry. On the one hand its non-dogmatic understanding of the diffused authority of reason, tradition and experience produces a unique climate for theology, and moreover one where even an 'exotic' like Cupitt might flourish.

> The Church of England was not blessed (or cursed, as the case may be) with a strong dogmatic tradition of its own . . . There was a distrust of 'hypothesis', needlessly elaborate speculation of a kind which was supposed to have flourished in the Middle Ages, and to be still flourishing on the European mainland. In a man like Locke, the influence of empiricist philosophy and natural science combined to form a strong preference for simplicity and economy in theorizing . . .

At its worst English theology has perhaps been too tentative and amateurish, but at its best it has been very responsive to new ideas in philosophy, science, and historical criticism, and has tried to stick closely to ascertainable facts and to moral experience.[68]

Yet on the other hand one suspects that theology is tolerated rather than encouraged by many within Anglicanism. The rigorous, post-enlightenment thinkers we meet in Cupitt's pages are unfamiliar. Cupitt describes the English as good only at natural science and imaginative literature.

We are too evasive and ironical to be capable of the pure and direct intellectual passion of a Pascal or a Nietzsche, preferring instead forms of expression in which we can veil ourselves . . . So when they had Hegel, we had Jane Austen.[69]

This is evident, for instance, in a particularly English theological compromise which for Cupitt is satisfyingly demolished by D. E. Nineham. This synthesis in British New Testament studies, represented by C. H. Dodd, T. W. Manson and Vincent Taylor (established by Westcott, Hort, Lightfoot and others in response to *Essays and Reviews* in the last century) is marked by the reading-back of developed orthodoxy into the New Testament.

For Anglicans it just had to be the case that a great scholar, fully up to German standards, could still become a great Bishop, without trauma . . . They adopted moderate critical orthodoxy with an almost audible sigh of relief. It promised to save their intellectual self-respect and their standing in the culture, and to do so without greatly changing the deep assumptions of the received faith.[70]

In this approach there is a qualified openness to biblical criticism, but no suggestion that critical theology might be called for as well. That is to say: doff the cap to the biblical scholar, but hold fast when the biblical roots of 'key doctrines' like the virgin birth or the physical resurrection are called into question.

So we can now see perhaps a little more clearly just what is Cupitt's position in England. His approach to theology is and is not typically Anglican. So Cupitt continues to function as an Anglican

priest and, being more committed to religion and to the worthwhile-
ness of the Christian programme than was, say, Michael Goulder, he
appears to be in no rush to resign his orders. There are those who
call for him to do so, of course, but there is little hope of a heresy trial
to enforce their wishes. The history of Anglican heresy trials has
been more embarrassing than shameful – who but the most
fundamentalist Christian would take umbrage at Bishop Colenso's
rather moderate views today? After all, in the autobiographical
snippets dotted throughout his work Cupitt again and again states
that history will be his judge.

Priest and prophet

Cupitt's Queens' College neighbour and regular sparring partner
Brian Hebblethwaite, in mildly denouncing him from the pulpit,
points out that the role of a priest is not to push his own views but
to represent the tradition of the community of faith which ordained
him and in which his identity resides. Yet upon reflection this has a
distinct sociological ring about it, recalling Peter Berger's definition of clergy as 'accredited reality definers'. So for Hebblethwaite
Cupitt must resign if he has ceased to believe and the church must
publicly denounce his views.[71] Yet it is not for nothing that
ordination is an indelible sacrament in the church catholic or that
the priest has traditionally been seen as God's servant first before
being the servant of the people. That is to say, priesthood has a
critical as well as an institutional, sociological dimension and those
whose view of a priest is that of a 'company man' would do well to
think again. Of course this is not to deny that there are limits, but I
shall proceed later in the chapter to argue that Cupitt is at least no
further beyond the pale than are the many other schools of thought
and individuals within the priesthood commonly considered to be
more orthodox.

Implicit in criticisms such as Hebblethwaite's is an understanding
of the role of priest and the role of prophet as quite distinct in the
history of religions. The popular conception of an Old Testament
prophet is perfectly captured by the figure of Nathan in the
Hollywood film *Solomon and Sheba*. Nathan would stand next to
Solomon, portrayed by Yul Brynner, with a constant expression of
far-away preoccupation. Yet Robert R. Wilson explodes this myth in

his elegant study *Prophecy and Society in Ancient Israel*.[72] He shows through a splendid methodology just how centrally located prophets often were in Israel, not infrequently as priests within the cult. The Hollywood image of the prophet lurking on the periphery must therefore be surrendered, as must the conception of the priest as an innocuous cultic functionary. After all, priests are in the Anglican ordinal charged to be 'messengers, watchmen and stewards of the Lord'. The original watchman, Ezekiel, certainly appears to have been a 'troubler of Israel', Cupitt in fact groups him alongside Jesus with the clowns and madmen in the Writings of Kierkegaard and Nietzsche, as the best sort of religious teacher.

Constructive theologian?

It is probably fair to say that Cupitt is as much an English philosopher of religion as a theologian, and this in part will explain his radical questionings. Dogmatic theologians do not normally draw their agendas from this source, nor work in this spirit. Yet again and again he appears consciously to don the mantle of the constructive theologian. He seems always to be about the business of improving Christian practice with his purges of the church's moral failures, sloppy mindedness and spiritual torpor with his sustained attacks on idols. In *Taking Leave of God* he describes the task of the theologian as the maintenance of spiritual continuity by constant doctrinal revision.[73] Even in the post-modern reaches of *The Long-Legged Fly* he sees the tradition as a river of signs which flows through us and must be freshly reinterpreted. At the beginning of that work he claims to be no longer interested in orthodoxy, yet laments that he appears fated to remain an ecclesiastical (rather than a post-ecclesiastical) theologian. He describes his task as reinterpreting Christian self-understanding in the light of the anti-philosophers.[74] This is not a common undertaking, as their systems are markedly unfriendly to the notions of 'being' which are highly favoured in Western thought and eagerly lit upon by theology. We have perhaps the clearest statement of it in a 1982 dialogue with John A. T. Robinson. Cupitt's aim is to continue reinterpreting:[75]

> I think I have done quite a lot constructively if I have done something in *Taking Leave of God* to save the essentials of

Christian spirituality, and in *The World to Come* to save something of the Christian doctrine of redemption, the old hope for a better world, and Christian ethics. So I rather congratulate myself on how constructive I have been.[76]

Bishop Robinson is at least sympathetic to this. In his review of *Taking Leave of God* he described it as a devotional book. But in the dialogue with Cupitt which I have already mentioned he commits himself further.

> In fact I found myself saying to Michael Green last term, who was being dismissive, 'Michael, you must listen to him. He is trying to do the sort of thing that Kierkegaard did for the church of his day a hundred years ago.'[77]

As I said in the Introduction, atheism is in the eyes of the beholder. For Cupitt, it is ' . . . a quasi-political smear word to brand innovators'.[78] We have already seen how Cupitt is quicker to demythologize doctrines than to throw them overboard, and we have just seen that his self-understanding is actually like that of the constructive theologian, albeit operating at higher altitudes and lower temperatures than normal. Perhaps his pleas deserve to be heard:

> It is only as it were within the context of the politics of faith, within the church context, that my views seem far out. If we looked at it in a larger context, I hope what I am doing would be regarded as constructive.[79]

'Let him who is without sin cast the first stone . . .'

There are many more subtle non-realists in the Anglican church today than there are honest radicals like Cupitt. Our pews are filled with adherents to a folk-religion who sometimes have little more than a nodding acquaintance with 'fully orthodox' Christianity. And among Anglican clergy, special interest groups cluster around such issues as women's ordination, social justice and opposition to liturgical reform, all to the exclusion of any hint of comprehensiveness. Why single Cupitt out?

To take a notable example, the clergy responsible for making Jung and Jungian-style spirituality fashionable in Anglican and Roman Catholic circles are either out-and-out non-realists or are wishing to have their cake and eat it. From their perspective God is an archetype, with no necessary existence outside the psyche. Yet outer and inner realms are often so effectively blurred in their discourse that no one suspects just what game is afoot.

Moreover Fergus Kerr, perhaps repenting of the evils done to Cupitt through past reviews in *New Blackfriars*, points out that many Roman Catholic clergy stay at their ecclesiastical posts while supporting positions not self-evidently more legitimate than Cupitt's. He mentions 'Christian Marxists' or those who interpret the world solely through the Marian revelations at Fatima (through *blue-tinted spectacles*, one feels compelled to add).

> In Britain, faced with Anglican eccentricities, Catholics are much inclined to preen themselves on the soundness of their doctrine – forgetting that a conversation with Catholics in Naples or Mexico or the Philippines or in Vatican City might easily reveal variations on the Catholic faith which are a great deal more bizarre and off-centre than anything any Anglican Chaplain at Cambridge is ever likely to produce.[80]

C. S. Lewis said somewhere that he would never condemn homosexual people or gamblers because he had never been tempted to take up either vice and could not say how he would react if ever he was. Yet Lewis was a particularly virulent and theologically reactionary hater of liberals. One suspects that he never stopped to consider the inconsistency of the two positions, for one can be certain that Lewis felt no temptation whatever to commit liberalism.

So those who occupy the earlier faith stages of *Life Lines* should pause if they feel drawn to condemn Cupitt and ask themselves how they might react in his position. Would they remain as faithful as Cupitt has been to the central themes of Christianity if cast into the modern nihil with the particular force with which he appears to have been?

Conclusion

I hope that I have demystified Don Cupitt somewhat in this study and offered a broader perspective on his more controversial views.

We have journeyed with him through nearly thirty years of developing theological thought, having noted initially the scientific and sceptical temper of mind and the youthful experiences out of which it arose. I delineated a long early period featuring the slow decline of theological realism before a developing philosophy of spirit: a philosophy of critical self-transcendence which called into question all human systems, dogmas and moral orders. The historical Jesus illustrated this principle for Cupitt and in fact continued to do so even after modern biblical criticism robbed him of some of these historical certainties in the late 1970s. His book *Taking Leave of God* rounded off this early period with a near complete departure from theological realism and its demythologizing into the radically Protestant and individualistic spirituality of 'Christian Buddhism'. A later period sought the implications of the anti-philosophers for Christianity: Nietzsche, Wittgenstein, Foucault, Derrida and others. The very recent books are struggling for a post-modern theology which will enable Christians to find an appropriate way forward to a better future promised in the message of Jesus and symbolized by the image of the exalted Christ. 'Here below' we are introduced to our new home in a world of intercommunicant subjectivity: two-dimensional, in which all meaning is incarnate. Here Cupitt has relaxed somewhat and become much more tolerant of religious world-views other than his own, now believing that all worlds are man-made.

I then made a variety of criticisms. I felt that Cupitt sold short many of the positions he opposed, and that sufficient hints of quasi-foundationalism remain, even in the later period, to support the old adage that 'Metaphysics buries its detractors.' I argued, too, that Cupitt undervalued developed dogma, except of course when he was busily demythologizing it so that the best features might survive. We saw that his is not a religion for everybody, as he effectively admits in his discussion of the various forms of the spiritual life in his book *Life Lines*. Key elements of Christian experience are certainly given short shrift in this 'tough religion of the will', such as love, depending, belonging and the primacy of 'gift' over 'task'. Nor does this seem to be an ideologically 'pure' religion, reflecting as it does a will-dominated puritanism and being implicated in the harsh and aggressive spirit of the modern capitalist world. In short, I feel that Cupitt should heed his own recent calls for deconstructive readings of theological texts, for that would force his own work to yield up its biases. Nevertheless, the contours of the later period which are still emerging, promise some resolution of these difficulties, so I do not intend my criticisms harshly. I would not by any means reject Cupitt's valuable contributions out of hand. I would prefer instead to echo the sentiments of Rowan Williams:

> Part of our difference is, I think, that Mr Cupitt actually cuts the Gordian knot of the 'objectivity' of God, where I should wish to go on tracing its several strands and trying to see why it has taken these particular contours.[1]

As to the suggestions that Cupitt is no Christian and should give up his priesthood, I have chosen to disagree. Much remains in his work from the Bible and the tradition, and he is both theocentric and christocentric in the form of his spirituality. Cupitt is no gnostic, no dissipated and religiously frivolous heretic, and does not confine himself to one or another religious 'hobby-horse' as do many 'orthodox' clergy and laity. He is a rigorous apologist for prophetic monotheism, for Christianity ranked first among the world religions, for taking the world seriously and for a proleptic eschatology in keeping with the best features of the tradition. He is a staunch advocate of an asceticism of mind, of moral seriousness and of the Anglican *via media* with its attendant virtue of 'practical divinity'. Indeed, Don Cupitt emerges as a distinctively Anglican apologist. He would not perhaps win as many converts to Christianity as would Billy Graham, but one suspects that he would far outstrip Graham's capacity to hold on to the church's intellectually disaffected fringe.

Don Cupitt remains a powerful voice for believers in a certain sort of modern crisis, long after more 'orthodox' voices have receded. 'He who has ears, let him hear . . .'

Bibliography

(a) The works of Don Cupitt 1961–1987

'What Do We Mean by "The Church"?', *Theology* 64, 1961, 275–81
'Four Arguments against The Devil', *Theology* 64, 1961, 413–15
'Reply to Attfield', *Theology* 64, 1961, 506
'What is the Gospel?' *Theology* 67, 1964, 343ff. (reprinted in *Explorations in Theology* 6, SCM Press 1979, 1–5)
'The Marrow Bone', *Frontier* 8, 1965, 92–5
'Theology and Practice', in *Crisis for Confirmation*, ed. M. Perry, SCM Press 1967
'Mansel's Theory of Regulative Truth', *Journal of Theological Studies* 18, 1967, 104–26
'The Doctrine of Analogy in the Age of Locke', *Journal of Theological Studies* 19, 1968, 186–202
'Transplanting the Heart', *Theology* 72, 1969, 341ff. (reprinted in *Explorations in Theology* 6, SCM Press 1979, 6–12)
'Mansel and Maurice on our Knowledge of God', *Theology* 73, 1970, 301–11
'What was Mansel Trying to Do?', *Journal of Theological Studies* 22, 1971, 544–7
Christ and the Hiddenness of God, Lutterworth Press 1971, second edition SCM Press 1985
'The Language of Eschatology: F. D. Maurice's Treatment of Heaven and Hell', *Anglican Theological Review* 54, 1972, 305ff. (reprinted in *Explorations in Theology* 6, SCM Press 1979, 13–26)
'God and the World in Post-Kantian Thought', *Theology* 75, 1972, 343–54
'The Resurrection: A Disagreement' (with C. F. D. Moule), *Theology* 75, 1972, 507–19 (reprinted in *Explorations in Theology* 6, SCM Press 1979, 27–41)
'One Jesus, Many Christs', in *Christ, Faith, and History*, ed. S. W. Sykes and J. P. Clayton, Cambridge University Press 1972, 78
Crisis of Moral Authority, Lutterworth Press 1972, second edition SCM Press 1985
'How We Make Moral Decisions', *Theology* 76, 1973, 239–50
'God and Morality', *Theology* 76, 1973, 356–64 (both this article and the

previous one later appeared in G. R. Dunstan, *Duty and Discernment*,
    SCM Press 1975, 76–100)
'Christian Existence in a Pluralist Society', *Theology* 77, 1974, 451–9
    (appended to the first edition of *The Leap of Reason*)
'Darwinism and English Religious Thought', *Theology* 78, 1975, 125ff.
    (reprinted in *Explorations in Theology* 6, SCM Press 1979, 42–9
'An Open Letter on Exorcism' (with G. W. H. Lampe) (reprinted in
    Explorations in Theology 6, SCM Press 1979, 50–3)
'The Meaning of Belief in God', *Cambridge Review* 96, 31 January 1975, 62f.
    (reprinted in *Explorations in Theology* 6, SCM Press 1979, 54–8)
'The Last Man', *BBC Radio 3*, 1975 (reprinted in *Explorations in Theology* 6,
    SCM Press 1979, 59–64)
'The Leap of Reason', *Theology* 78, 1975, 291–302 (appended to the first
    edition of *The Leap of Reason*)
'The Finality of Christ', *Theology* 78, 1975, 618–28 (appended to the first
    edition of *The Leap of Reason*)
'Natural Evil', in *Man and Nature*, ed. Hugh Montefiore, Collins 1975
'Some Evidence from Other Relgions', ibid.
'God and the Futures of Man', ibid.
'Christ Ethics Today', *Crucible*, July/Sept 1976, 104–7
'And Behold, a Multitude', *The Listener*, 18 March 1976, 332f.
'The Original Jesus', *The Listener*, 15 July 1976, 45f.
'The Charismatic Illusion', *The Listener*, 22 July 1976, 77f.
'The Church Against the State, *The Listener*, 29 July 1976, 110f.
'Where is Heaven Now?', *The Listener*, 5 August 1976, 146f.
The Leap of Reason, Sheldon Press 1976, second edition SCM Press 1985
The Worlds of Science and Religion, Sheldon Press 1976
'Man, Bound and Free', *Theology* 80, 1977, 100ff. (reprinted in *Explorations
    in Theology* 6, SCM Press 1979, 79–86)
'The Christ of Christendom', in *The Myth of God Incarnate*, ed. John Hick,
    SCM Press 1977, 133–47
'A Final Comment', ibid., 205f.
✻ *Who Was Jesus?* (with Peter Armstrong), BBC Publications 1977
'Myth Understood', *Theology* 81, 1978, 417ff. (reprinted in *Explorations in
    Theology* 6, SCM Press 1979, 70–8)
'Whither Personal Ethics?', *The Modern Churchman* 21, 1978, 72ff.
    (reprinted under the title 'Critical Christian Ethics' in *Explorations in
    Theology* 6, SCM Press 1979, 87–97)
'The Ethics of this World and the Ethics of the World to Come', (reprinted
    in *Explorations in Theology* 6, SCM Press 1979, 98–109)
Explorations in Theology 6, SCM Press 1979
'Jesus and the Meaning of God', in *Incarnation and Myth*, ed. Michael
    Goulder, SCM Press 1979, 31–40

'Mr Hebblethwaite on the Incarnation', ibid., 43–6

'Professor Stanton on Incarnational Language in the New Testament', ibid., 166–9

The Nature of Man, Sheldon Press 1979

✝ *The Debate About Christ*, SCM Press 1979

✝ *Jesus and the Gospel of God*, Lutterworth Press 1979

'The Paradoxical Pontiff', *The Times Literary Supplement*, 25 April 1980, 458

Review of Jürgen Moltmann, *The Future of Creation*, *Theology* 83, 1980, 215f.

Taking Leave of God, SCM Press 1980

'Response to the Review by D. L. Edwards', *Theology* 84, 1981, 199ff.

'Reinterpreting Christianity' *Cambridge Review*, 7 February 1981, 92–6

'Turbulent Trappist' *The Times Literary Supplement*, 13 February 1981, 156

'On the side of the Angels', *The Times Literary Supplement*, 7 August 1981, 902

'Kant and the Negative Theology', in *The Philosophical Frontiers of Christian Theology*, ed. Brian Hebblethwaite and Stewart Sutherland, Cambridge University Press 1982

The World to Come, SCM Press 1982

'Religion and Critical Thinking (1 and 2)', *Theology* 86, 1983, 243–9, 328–35 (slightly reworded, these articles are in *The Sea of Faith*, 249–60)

'Thought Crimes in the Church', *The Listener*, 5 July 1984, 4

'A Reply to Rowan Williams', *Modern Theology* 1, 1984, 25–31

The Sea of Faith, BBC Publications 1984

(The following series of five articles were entitled 'A Future for Religious Thought?'. They are reprinted in the appendix to *Only Human*).

'Religion without Superstition', *The Listener*, 13 September 1984, 5f.

'Religion without Dogma', *The Listener*, 20 September 1984, 5f. 21

'Life after Life after Death', *The Listener*, 27 September 1984, 17

'The Struggle against Theological Realism', *The Listener*, 4 October 1984, 17

'The Second Disenchantment', *The Listener*, 11 October 1984, 9

'*The Sea of Faith*: The Backwash', *The Listener*, 1 November 1984, 24

Only Human, SCM Press 1985

'A Sense of History', *Theology* 89, 1986, 362–6

Life Lines, SCM Press 1986

The Long-Legged Fly, SCM Press 1987

'A Tale of Two Cities: The World to Come' (with J. A. T. Robinson) in J. A. T. Robinson, *Where Three Ways Meet*, ed. Eric James, SCM Press 1987

(b)   Book reviews and responses

Christ and the Hiddenness of God
   Some Reviews

H. Roberts, *The Expository Times* 83, 1971, 58f.
M. France, *Frontier* 15, 1972, 119f.
R. McKinney, *Theology* 75, 1972, 543ff.
J. I. Packer, *The Churchman* 88, 1974, 59f.
   A Response

P. Carnley, *The Structure of Resurrection Belief*, Clarendon Press 1987, 163–82

Crisis of Moral Authority
   Some Reviews

M. France, *Frontier* 16, 1973, 53f.
L. De Wolf, *Interpretation* 27, 1973, 378
W. Muelder, *Christian Century* 90, 1973, 296
J. Fraser, *Scottish Journal of Theology* 26, 1973, 497ff.
S. Quitsland, *Catholic Biblical Quarterly* 35, 1973, 371ff.
P. Simmons, *Review and Expositor* 71, 1974, 121f.
C. Milton, *The Expository Times* 86, 1974, 2f.
J. I. Packer, *The Churchman* 88, 1974, 60f.

The Leap of Reason
   Some Reviews

D. Allen, *Theology Today* 34, 1977, 340f.
J. Thomas, *The Expository Times* 88, 1977, 156
M. Wiles, *Journal of Theological Studies* 28, 1977, 265ff.
J. McIntyre, *Scottish Journal of Theology* 30, 1977, 576–81
R. Griffiths, *The Evangelical Quarterly* 49, 1977, 125f.
R. Cunningham, *Review and Expositor* 75, 1978, 150ff.
R. Laura, *International Journal of Philosophy and Religion* 11, 1980, 68f.

The Worlds of Science and Religion
   A Review
M. Cook, *Zygon* 14, 1979, 189

Who Was Jesus?
   A Review
K. Grayston, *Theology* 82, 1979, 60–2

The Nature of Man
   Some Reviews
G. Slater, *The Expository Times* 90, 1979, 92

G. Carey, *The Churchman* 94, 1980, 77f.
H. O. Jones, *Theology* 84, 1981, 123f.

Jesus and the Gospel of God
    Some Reviews

J. Drury, *Theology* 82, 1979, 377ff.
C. Rodd, *The Expository Times* 90, 1979, 321f.
G. Turner, *New Blackfriars* 60, 1979, 416–25
R. Crawford, *The Evangelical Quarterly* 52, 1980, 62f.

The Debate about Christ
    Some Reviews

N. Wright, *The Churchman* 93, 1979, 351
R. Banks, *St Mark's Review* 102, 1980, 44f.
F. Kerr, *Journal of Theological Studies* 31, 1980, 282f.
J. Mackey, *Theology* 83, 1980, 217f.
R. Hoffmann, *Journal of Ecumenical Studies* 19, 1982, 803f.

Explorations in Theology 6
    Some Reviews

C. Baxter, *The Churchman* 94, 1980, 163
H. Jones, *Theology* 84, 1981, 123

Taking Leave of God
    Some Reviews

D. L. Edwards, 'Atheist Priest?' *Church Times*, 3 October 1980, 7
J. A. T. Robinson, 'Man's Last and Highest Parting', *The Times Literary Supplement*, 5 December 1980
James Mark, *Theology* 84, 1981, 211ff.
G. Slater, *The Expository Times* 92, 1981, 154
R. Masson, *Horizons* 10, 1983, 387f.
    Some Responses

F. Kerr, 'Cupitt's Dogmas', *New Blackfriars* 62, 1981, 204–14
Keith Ward, *Holding Fast To God*, SPCK 1982
    Reponses to Cupitt and Ward

C. Longley, 'Does God Exist? Faith Gets a Lift', *The Times*, 12 January 1983, 10
S. Sutherland, 'A Theological Fable', *Kings Theological Review* 6, 1983, 17ff.

The World to Come
    Some Reviews

S. Collins, *Theology* 86, 1983, 46ff.
G. Slater, *The Expository Times* 94, 1983, 188

The Sea of Faith
   Some Reviews

D. Oliphant, *St Mark's Review*, 123/124, 1985, 74ff.

M. Wiles, *Theology* 88, 1985, 232f.

   Some Responses

D. Cupitt, '*The Sea of Faith:* The Backwash', *The Listener*, 1 November 1984, 24

F. Kerr, 'Don Cupitt's Philosophy', *The Month* 267, 1985, 87–90

B. Hebblethwaite, 'What Are We To Think About Don Cupitt?', in *Preaching Through the Christian Year* 10, Mowbray 1985

Only Human
   A Review

K. Surin, *Theology* 89, 1986, 134ff.

Life Lines
   A Review

F. Kerr, *New Blackfriars* 68, 1987, 363f.

(c) Other responses

D. G. Attfield, 'Reply to Cupitt's Four Arguments against the Devil', *Theology* 64, 1961, 461f.

A. Herbert, J. Lawrence and T. Simpson, 'Letters to the Editor: The Resurrection, A Disagreement', *Theology* 75, 1972, 507–19

D. Brindley and H. Oppenheimer, 'Myth Understood' (in 'Letters to the Editor') *Theology* 82, 1979, 123–6

C. Gunton, 'The Political Christ: Some Reflections on Mr Cupitt's Thesis', *Scottish Journal of Theology* 32, 1979, 521–40

N. Lash, 'Jesus and the Meaning of "God" – a Comment', in *Incarnation and Myth*, ed. M. Goulder, SCM Press 1979, 41–3

G. Stanton, Mr Cupitt on 'Incarnational Christology in the New Testament', in ibid., 170–3

R. Pelly, D. L. Edwards and D. Cupitt, 'Letters to the Editor on "Atheism"', *Theology* 84, 1981, 199–201

F. Dunlop, 'In Defence of Orthodoxy: Interpreting Don Cupitt', *Religious Studies* 18, 1982, 201–10

J. Hick, 'The Wider God Debate', in J. Hick and M. Goulder, *Why Believe in God?*, SCM Press 1983, 97–111

P. Mullen, 'Serial Theology', *Theology* 86, 1983, 25–9

R. Williams, 'Religious Realism: On Not Quite Agreeing with Don Cupitt', *Modern Theology* 1, 1984, 3–24

M. Matthews, 'Cupitt's Context', *New Blackfriars* 66, 1985, 533–43

B. Russell, 'With Respect to Don Cupitt', *Theology* 88, 1985, 5–11

D. A. Walker, 'Truth and Objectivity: A Response to Don Cupitt', *The Expository Times* 97, 1985, 75–9

D. Cohn-Sherbok, 'Don Cupitt and Reconstructionist Judaism', *Theology* 89, 1986, 436–40

C. Pickstone, 'Mondrian, Don Cupitt, and the Cheshire Cat: An Adventure in Wonderland', *Theology* 89, 1986, 187–94

D. Turner, 'De-Centring Theology', *Modern Theology* 2, 1986, 125–43

W. Schwarz, 'Our Father Which Art on Earth', *The Guardian*, 21 September 87, 21

Notes

For bibliographical details of books and articles by or about Don Cupitt see the bibliography.

Preface

1. Walter Schwarz. 'Our Father Who Art on Earth', *The Guardian*, 21 September 1987, 21.
2. Dust jacket of *Crisis of Moral Authority* (1972).
3. *Church Times*, 3 October 1980.

Biographical Sketch

1. 'How We Make Moral Decisions', *Theology* 76, 1973, 244.
2. 'The Church against the State', *The Listener*, 29 July 1976, 110.
3. 'Designer Realism', see *Life Lines*, 92.
4. *Crisis of Moral Authority* (second edition 1985), 9.
5. *Explorations in Theology* 6, viii.
6. 'Doctrinal Realism', 'Obedientary Realism', *Life Lines*, 92 (cf. 69).
7. Preface to *Christ and the Hiddenness of God* (second edition, 1985), 5.
8. *Explorations in Theology* 6, viii.
9. *Christ and the Hiddenness of God* (second edition, 1985), 5f.
10. Ibid.
11. *The Sea of Faith*, 22.
12. Ibid., 33f. and passim.
13. *Life Lines*, 93.
14. Preface to *The Leap of Reason* (second edition, 1985).
15. Schwarz, 'Our Father' (Preface, n. 1 above).
16. In *Why Believe in God?*, ed. John Hick and Michael Goulder, 1–29.
17. *Taking Leave of God*, 30f.
18. *Life Lines*, 31f.
19. *Christ and the Hiddenness of God* (second edition), 9.

I. The Early Cupitt

1. See e.g. Cupitt's review of J. Moltmann, *The Future of Creation*, *Theology* 1980, 215f.
2. See e.g. 'Mr Hebblethwaite on the Incarnation', in *Incarnation and Myth*, ed. Michael Goulder, SCM Press 1979, 44f.

3. 'What Do We Mean by "The Church"?', *Theology* 1961.

4. In 'One Jesus, Many Christs', *Christ, Faith and History*, ed. Stephen Sykes.

5. 'What is the Gospel?', *Theology* 1964.

6. 'Mansel's Theory of Regulative Truth', *Journal of Theological Studies* 1967, 121.

7. Ibid., 117.

8. *Christ and the Hiddenness of God* (second edition 1985), 213.

9. *The Leap of Reason* (second edition 1985), 77f.

10. 'Mansel and Maurice on our Knowledge of God', *Theology* 1970, 311.

11. *Crisis of Moral Authority* (second edition 1985), 155.

12. *Explorations in Theology* 6, ix.

13. Ibid., 57f.

14. 'God and the Futures of Man', in *Man and Nature*, ed. Hugh Montefiore, 194.

15. *The Worlds of Science and Religion*, 31.

16. Ibid., 109.

17. 'Natural Evil', in *Man and Nature*, 120.

18. *The Leap of Reason* (second edition), 75.

19. 'One Jesus, Many Christs', in *Christ, Faith and History*, 137.

20. 'The Original Jesus', *The Listener* 1976, 46.

21. *The Debate about Christ*, 114.

22. 'A Tale of Two Cities', with John A. T. Robinson, in: John A. T. Robinson, *Where Three Ways Meet*, ed. Eric James, SCM Press 1987, 30.

23. *Christ and the Hiddenness of God* (second edition), 8.

24. 'How We Make Moral Decisions' and 'God and Morality', *Theology* 1973.

25. Originally published as 'Whither Personal Ethics?', *The Modern Churchman* 1978.

26. See *Explorations in Theology* 6, xi.

27. 'A Reply to Rowan Williams', *Modern Theology* 1984, 27.

28. In the introduction to *Explorations in Theology* 6 and the prefaces to 1985 editions of earlier works.

29. 'A Reply to Rowan Williams', 27.

30. Denys Turner, 'De-Centring Theology', *Modern Theology* 1986, 126.

31. Fergus Kerr, 'Cupitt's Dogmas', *New Blackfriars* 1981, 210.

32. *Taking Leave of God*, 99.

33. Ibid., 136.

34. Ibid., 69.

35. Ibid., xii.

36. Steven Collins, review of *The World to Come*, *Theology* 1983, 47.

37. Rowan Williams, 'Religious Realism: On Not Quite Agreeing with Don Cupitt', *Modern Theology* 1984, 4.

38. Answering R. Pelly in the reply to David L. Edwards' review of *Taking Leave of God*, in 'Letters to the Editor on Atheism', *Theology* 1981, 201.

39. 'Where is Heaven Now?', *The Listener*, 5 August 1976, 146.

40. 'Four Arguments against the Devil', *Theology* 1961, 413.

41. *Explorations in Theology* 6, vii, referring to 'What is the Gospel?' (n. 5 above).

42. 'God and Morality', *Theology* 1973.

43. *The Debate about Christ*, 144.

44. *Who Was Jesus?*, 92.

45. 'Professor Stanton on Incarnational Language in the New Testament', in *Incarnation and Myth*, 169.

46. *Jesus and the Gospel of God*, 18.

47. Ibid., 73.

48. 'What Do We Mean by "The Church"?' (n. 3 above), 278.

49. 'Christian Existence in a Pluralist Society', *Theology* 1974, 459.

50. 'The Church against the State', *The Listener*, 29 July 1976, 111.

51. 'The Paradoxical Pontiff', *The Times Literary Supplement*, 25 April 1980, 458.

52. 'Thought Crimes in the Church', *The Listener*, 5 July 1984, 4.

II. The Later Cupitt

1. *The World to Come*, xiv.

2. *Only Human*, 194.

3. See e.g. *The World to Come*, 104.

4. *The Sea of Faith*, 18.

5. See e.g. ibid., 164.

6. 'Religion and Critical Thinking 2', *Theology* 1983, 329.

7. J. A. T. Robinson, *Where Three Ways Meet*, 31.

8. 'A Reply to Rowan Williams' (Chapter I, n. 27 above), 27.

9. *The World to Come*, 136f.

10. Ibid., 143.

11. Ibid., 159.

12. *Where Three Ways Meet*, 24.

13. The page numbers cited in the text are from the book, not the articles.

14. *Where Three Ways Meet*, 24.

15. Schwarz, 'Our Father' (Preface, n. 1 above), 21.

III. Cupitt in Retrospect: Credibility, Adequacy, Orthodoxy

1. 'Religion without Superstition', *The Listener*, 13 September 1984, 5.

2. G. Turner, review of *Jesus and the Gospel of God*, *New Blackfriars* 1979, 425.

3. Brian Hebblethwaite, 'What are We to Think of Don Cupitt?', in *Preaching through the Christian Year 10*, Mowbray 1985, 161.

4. G. Slater, review of *The World to Come*, *The Expository Times* 1983, 188.

5. *Where Three Ways Meet*, 27.

6. John Macquarrie, *Principles of Christian Theology*, SCM Press 1966.

7. See e.g. Rowan Williams, 'Religious Realism' (Chapter I, n. 37 above), 4.

8. As is the case, for instance, in Cupitt's 1984 response to Rowan Williams (Chapter I, n. 27 above).

9. 'Kant and the Negative Theology', in *The Philosophical Frontiers of Christian Theology*, ed. Brian Hebblethwaite and Stewart Sutherland (1982), 59.

10. Keith Ward, *Holding Fast to God*, SPCK 1982, 142.

11. John A. T. Robinson, 'Man's Last and Highest Parting', *The Times Literary Supplement*, 5 December 1980; John Hick, *Why Believe in God?*, 107.

12. F. Kerr, 'Cupitt's Dogmas' (Chapter I, n. 31 above), 211.

13. Rowan Williams (n. 7 above), 7.

14. Peter Berger, *The Social Reality of Religion*, Penguin Books 1973, 183.

15. *The Long-Legged Fly*, 145f.

16. Brian Russell, 'With Respect to Don Cupitt', *Theology* 1985, 7.

17. Fergus Kerr, *Theology after Wittgenstein*; his point here is also made in his 'Cupitt's Dogmas' (Chapter I, n. 31 above).

18. D. A. Walker, 'Truth and Objectivity: A Response to Don Cupitt', *The Expository Times* 1985, 78.

19. Maurice Wiles, review of *The Sea of Faith*, Theology 1985, 233.

20. R. Griffiths, review of *The Leap of Reason*, *The Evangelical Quarterly* 1977, 126.

21. Wiles, review of *The Leap of Reason*, *Journal of Theological Studies*, 1977, 266.

22. *Taking Leave of God*, 96.

23. *Life Lines*, 222.

24. Ward, *Holding Fast* (n. 10 above), 58.

25. E.g. James Mark, review of *Taking Leave of God*, *Theology* 1981, 212.

26. *Taking Leave of God*, 9.

27. Ward, *Holding Fast*, 60.

28. See e.g. John Macquarrie, *In Search of Humanity*, SCM Press 1982, ch. xi.

29. Rowan Williams, 'Religious Realism', 13.

30. F. W. Dillistone, *Religious Experience and Christian Faith*, SCM Press 1981, ch. 5.

31. Edward Schillebeeckx, *Jesus in Our Western Culture*, SCM Press 1987, 5.

32. *Taking Leave of God*, 132f.

33. Ward, *Holding Fast*, 60.

34. Ibid., 79, 152.

35. D. Dubarle, 'Buddhist Spirituality and the Christian Understanding of God', *Concilium* 116, 1979, 67.

36. E.g. *Only Human*, 49; *The Long-Legged Fly*, 147.

37. G. Turner (n. 2 above), 422ff.

38. Sebastian Moore, *The Fire and the Rose are One*, Darton, Longman and Todd 1980, ch. 32.

39. Graham Stanton, 'Mr Cupitt on Incarnational Theology in the New Testament', in *Incarnation and Myth*.

40. R. Hoffman, review of *The Debate about Christ*, *Journal of Ecumenical Studies*, 1982, 804.

41. *The World to Come*, ch. 5.

42. *The Debate about Christ*, 92.

43. James Mackey, review of *The Debate about Christ*, *Theology* 1980, 218.

44. Ward, *Holding Fast*, 25.

45. Helen Oppenheimer, 'Myth Understood', *Theology* 1979, 126.

46. Sebastian Moore, *The Fire and the Rose*, 138.

47. Helen Oppenheimer (see n. 45).

48. As suggested in *The World to Come*, 95.

49. Melvyn Matthews, 'Cupitt's Context', *New Blackfriars* 1985, 539.

50. Rowan Wiliams, 'Religious Realism', part 3.

51. *The Leap of Reason*, 89.

52. Rowan Williams, 'Religious Realism', 20.

53. Schwarz, 'Our Father' (Preface, n. 1 above).

54. John Bowker, *The Sense of God*, Clarendon Press 1973, 19.

55. Rowan Williams, 'Religious Realism', 21.

56. Ibid., 20.

57. E.g. Melvyn Matthews (n. 49), 538.

58. Rowan Williams, 'Religious Realism', 10f.

59. See David E. Jenkins, *The Contradiction of Christianity*, SCM Press 1976.

60. Fergus Kerr, 'Cupitt's Dogmas', 208; cf. Ward, *Holding Fast*, 52.

61. Peter Mullen, 'Serial Theology', *Theology* 1983, 27f.

62. Dan Cohn-Sherbok, 'Don Cupitt and Reconstructionist Judaism', *Theology* 1986, 436–40.

63. Rowan Williams, 'Religious Realism', 21f.; D. Turner, 'De-Centring Theology' (Chapter I, n. 30 above), 135.

64. Fergus Kerr, 'Cupitt's Dogmas', 210.

65. Charles Pickstone, 'Mondrian, Don Cupitt and the Cheshire Cat: An Adventure in Wonderland', *Theology* 1986, 190.

66. Ibid., 191.

67. David L. Edwards, 'Atheist Priest', *Church Times*, 3 October 1980, 7.

68. *The Debate about Christ*, viii.

69. 'The Sea of Faith: The Backwash', *The Listener*, 1 November 1984, 24.

70. Don Cupitt, 'A Sense of History', *Theology* 1986, 366.

71. Hebblethwaite, 'What are We to Think of Don Cupitt?'.

72. Robert R. Wilson, *Prophecy and Society in Ancient Israel*, Fortress Press 1980.

73. *Taking Leave of God*, ch. 6.

74. *The World to Come*, xvi.

75. In John A. T. Robinson, *Where Three Ways Meet*, 19.

76. Ibid., 32.

77. Ibid., 25.

78. *The Sea of Faith*, 224.

79. *Where Three Ways Meet*, 32.

80. Fergus Kerr, 'Cupitt's Dogmas', 204.

Conclusion

1. Rowan Williams, 'Religious Realism', 22.

Index